Dreams:

Discover the Meaning of Your Dreams and How to Dream What You Want - Dream Interpretation, Lucid Dreaming, and Dream Psychology

Table of Contents

Discover the Meaning of Your Dreams and How to Dream What You Want - Dream Interpretation, Lucid Dreaming, and Dream Psychology without the consent of the author or copyright owner. Legal action will be pursued if this is breached.

Disclaimer Notice:

Please note the information contained within this document is for educational and entertainment purposes only. Every attempt has been made to provide accurate, up to date and reliable complete information. No warranties of any kind are expressed or implied. Readers acknowledge that the author is not engaging in the rendering of legal, financial, medical or professional advice.

Bonus

Who can dream without a good night's sleep? Learn ways to sleep better, quickly! As my passion is sharing valuable information that tangibly impacts your life (be it learning how to dream properly or otherwise), I'd like to invite you to the free bonus below to positively affect your life in other dimensions, and join my mailing list where I drip-feed free information that I think may be of benefit to you (zero spam ever).

If you want to take your health to the next level, I recommend the free resource below for some easy-to-follow quick tips that make a huge impact.

23 Health Tips & Hacks You Probably Aren't Doing But Should Be to Reduce Fatigue, Improve Sleep and Recovery, Boost Sex Drive, and Heal Your Gut

Visit https://publishfs.leadpages.co/getultrahealth/

Introduction

Thank you for purchasing the book, *Dreams: Discover the Meaning of your Dreams and how to Dream what you want – Dream Interpretation, Lucid Dreaming and Dream Psychology.*

Every one of us spends close to an hour and a half to two hours each night experiencing the mystery of dreaming, as we sleep. Images, fantastical landscapes, secret rooms and hallways that lead nowhere are arrayed in images that speak to us from our subconscious world. This is a world we're not normally aware of, but in sleep it comes to life, filling our sleeping minds with the psychological flotsam of our experiences.

We all have multiple dreams that may last for a minimum of ten minutes to a maximum of forty-five minutes. When we wake up, we realize we remember very few details about our dreams. But have you ever woken up in the middle of the night and exclaimed to yourself that you just had the craziest dream? Have you wondered what it meant?

Why was that pink poodle having blue puppies? Why did Boris Yeltsin appear in the form of a white wolf, floating down from the sky, to land on the back porch? And why (for heaven's sake), did you tell him to be careful? Did Bill Clinton really smoke a cigar in your kitchen, even after you politely asked him not to? More importantly, was it *just* a cigar, or did it symbolize something else?

And sometimes, friends, a cigar is just a cigar. In dreams, though, a cigar can me many things, regardless of who's smoking it. Your mom, your cat, your budgie, or your deceased landlord may be chomping on that stogie in the land of dreams. Some dreams can certainly have us scratching our heads, but that's why we're here. We're to learn how to interpret our dreams and possibly, to learn how to direct them through the application of lucid dreaming.

Dreams are said to be the poems we've subconsciously written to describe the painful and puzzling emotions that swirl behind your immediate awareness. We lead challenging lives that give us little time for introspection and reflection. That means we can be out of touch with our feelings and can't seem to find the time to process them, where they came from, or how we can resolve feelings which haven't been adequately acknowledged. Taking time to be touch with our emotions has fallen from post-modern grace and we're all that much poorer for it.

But dreams have the power to help us find balance in the rush and noise of life and provide us with an opportunity to re-connect with ourselves. In seeking to better understand our dreams, we are allowed the chance to establish contact with the deepest level of our intellects. Our sub-conscious mind is part of who we are and acknowledging it's there and seeking out the wisdom and revelations it can make possible, can serve the role of salve to our modern dysfunction. By reading the poems our subconscious writes and reads to us as we sleep, we can find out so much more about who we are as people and again find the fullness of what it means to be intentionally and actively human in what is rapidly becoming a post-emotional world.

You can learn to be fed by your dreams and to use them as tools for allowing your subconscious mind to approach the problems and difficult challenges you've been trying to tackle or overcome in your waking life. With the help of dream analysis, you'll be able to come to a more finely-tuned understanding of your reactions to the world around you and therefore, be enabled to approach life with greater equanimity and less anxiety. Instead of bashing our heads against the brick wall of life, we can call on our dreams to read us the poem our subconscious mind has written and from that deep, emotional place, learn to face what we must, armed with information we might otherwise not have access to. This is the information our conscious minds ignore in their efforts to retain information deemed more important to us than our psychological nuances. But those nuances genuinely matter. They're part of your overall health and your ability to cope with daily life. They're also the key to your success in relationships with others, at work, at home and in the greater world around you.

Because the subconscious doesn't function in the same straightforward, logical way our conscious minds do while

we're awake, its messages to us are more fluid and
decidedly more obtuse. The blurred lines inherent to this
part of our intellects present a different lens through which
to see our problems, emotions and challenges.   By
presenting us with symbols and scenes that play out in our
sleep, the subconscious mind is writing us prescriptions
for action. It's also writing us prescriptions to feel more at
peace with what we experience, and a way to process those
things which might otherwise disturb us beyond our
capacity to endure them. This allows us to tackle problems
by seeing them from a more fluid perspective, not
accessible to us in waking life. Waking consciousness
won't allow for that kind of thinking. It's too busy doing
that "life thing" and processing information logically and
analytically. In dreams, the only analytical component is
that which the dreamer applies in the project of
interpreting what's been seen in them – and that part
comes once you're awake.

Dreams can confirm an intuition or instinct that has been
on the edge of your consciousness while engrossed in the
business of living. They can also point to what is really
important to you (through your memories) so that you're
able to leave behind or disregard a memory that may have
seemed important, but doesn't actually hold any great
significance for you.   That memory might even be
preventing you from moving forward in life and getting the
most from its many gifts.

But dreams can also be a cut and dried accumulation of
muddled,   random   thoughts   and   memories   spliced

together, as they've already received so much active attention from you in the waking world. These dreams usually don't have any meaning at all; they are simply sub-intellectual salad of impressions; an instant replay of the day's events, courtesy of your subconscious. But have you ever wondered why you've had a specific dream? This book will help you answer some questions you may have had all your life about dreams, their nature and what they have to teach you about yourself. It can also help you distinguish between dreams you should probably pay special attention to, in terms of their value and those which are less significant.

I'm going to explain a range of different theories that have emerged over the last few decades concerning dreams. These theories have helped psychologists understand and interpret the significance of dreams people often have, providing insight into common psychological realities and the human way of dealing with them as we sleep. Dreams shared in common by many people have many similar characteristics and features. These range from the mundane to the fantastical and sometimes various combinations of both.

Many dreams have distinct meanings and these can vary from person to person, while sharing features like flying, appearing naked in public, or being chased down dark hallways. There are myriad symbols that feature in almost every living person's dreams. The connection between a few of these symbols and your life will be explained. I'll explain the universal meaning of some of the more prevalent dream symbols. This will give you a better idea about how you can interpret your dreams. The semiotics of the dream world is a fascinating study and this book is just the tip of the iceberg. I hope it will encourage you to strike out on your own and investigate the world of dreams and the symbols which often appear in them, yourself. There's a deep well of self-knowledge to be drunk from in the study of dream interpretation.

We're also going to explore the idea of lucid dreaming, which is a type of psychological art. If you are able to dream lucidly, you'll be able to control the way your dream unfolds. You will also be able to control every aspect of your dream. It has been proven scientifically that lucid dreaming exists and that it's possible for everyone, given concentration and consistent, sustained effort. This book provides you with techniques to help you understand how you can dream lucidly, too.

You may be very keen on interpreting your dreams. You may have a million questions in your mind when you've woken up right after a particularly puzzling, strange dream. There may also have been times you've woken up in the middle of the night because of a dream that scared you. At times like those, you shouldn't go back to sleep. Instead stay awake and write down everything you remember about the dream, so that when you wake up in the morning, you can try to interpret its meaning. Keep this book nearby as well, as it will become a valuable and immediate reference as you learn to interpret your dreams.

Thank you for purchasing the book. I hope you find its contents informative and helpful. Let's enter the world of dreams and find out more about them.

Chapter 1: Chasing our Elusive Dreams

Dreams are psychological phenomena that humans have sought to understand since we started having them and wondering about them. They may seem weird, strange or even terrifying. However, you've probably always pondered the meaning of your dreams, or what happened in your life to provoke them. You may believe they have a role in maintaining the psychological and physical health of your body. This may be true to an extent. There are many theories about the purpose and potential health benefits of dreams. Despite that, there's an entire school of psychological examination which believes that dreams serve no purpose at all.

The interpretation of our dreams and nightmares have been a source of fascination for human beings since the point in our development at which we began to understand that our lives were finite. Since the dawn of our lives as sentient beings, we've sought to understand the sometimes strange and perplexing night time world that plays out in our heads, as we sleep. All over the world, history's record is witness to our long term study of dreams and what they mean. Let's explore the evolution of the study of dreams and how it's evolved through the ages.

The historical evolution of dream interpretation

The Hindu Upanishads, written three thousand years ago, describe dreams as the expression of a higher human consciousness, in which we are at our most divine. Similar concepts of the role of dreaming in human consciousness are found throughout the Ancient East. Many world cultures and religious systems have described dreams as our means of receiving direct communication from God. The Hebrew Scriptures are also filled with accounts of dreams which manifest the will of the Creator, instructing the chosen dreamers to perform certain actions on the part of God.

Ancient cultures generally held to the belief that some dreams were important enough to seek the interpretative services of local temple clergy. They also believed that subsequent dreams would reveal the meaning of previous ones, which they were seeking the full meaning of. In the higher consciousness of the dream world, the ancients believed they were being sent direct messages from the realm of godhead and, for this reason, took at least some of their dreams very seriously. Cultures like those which existed in Babylon also believed there was little distinction between life in their waking moments, and the life they experienced in dreams. Presciently, they saw dreams as an extension of their daily lives that served to illuminate them, making the experience of living even richer. They instinctively sensed this was the case, without knowing anything about the existence of the subconscious, as we understand it today.

Most famously, the Babylonians gave us the Epic of Gilgamesh (circa 2100 BCE), in which the hero's dream is detailed as an odyssey (a type of vision quest) in the form of an epic poem. While not an interpretative text, the symbolism forms at least part of the ancient canon which established the semiotic basis for modern dream interpretation. Gilgamesh is also considered to be the world's original work of literature and the original context of some of the stories which appear in the Bible (the Flood Narrative, in particular). Archaeologists continue to explore the possibility that Gilgamesh was a living person on whom the Epic was based.

As long as 5,000 years ago, at about the same time the Upanishads were written, the ancient Sumerians similarly codified their cultural ideas about dreams. This is the earliest layer of the recorded history of dream interpretation. The people of this Mesopotamian society also believed that the soul of the dreamer left its body while dreaming (an early reference to what some call astral projection, today). This ancient culture was the first to compile universal symbols encountered in dreams and to interpret them in a systematic manner. This system was primarily used by priests specifically appointed to the task of interpreting the dreams of those who came to them, seeking answers. They served as intermediaries between the gods (believed to be the originators of dreams) and Sumerian dreamers. It's from this ancient tradition that

3

historians claim other systems of dream analysis spread through the ancient world. This means the Sumerian system was an early influence on dreams which appear in the Hebrew and Christian scriptures (which we'll discuss a little later on) and also in Arabic and Greek interpretative traditions. They would also have been a strong influence on the Egyptian Book of Dreams (see below).

The practice of incubation was common to many ancient cultures, in one form or another. This would entail sleeping in a holy place after having encountered a dream of notable significance and also, interpretation by a priestess, priest or Shaman. The dreamer would, with ritual support, pray for a supplemental dream to illuminate the true meaning of one they'd had earlier. Any subsequent dream would then be interpreted in light of the first.

Oneiromancy (dream divination) is also the subject of the Egyptian Book of Dreams, a papyrus dating from the time of Egyptian Pharaoh, Rameses II (1279-1213, BCE). The papyrus is an early example of dream interpretation (following the example of the influential Sumerian system), listing types of dreams and the symbols they feature, together with diagnoses as to whether the dream in question was considered or "good" or "bad", via interpretation of the symbols involved. This categorization is first seen in the Mesopotamian model and was taken up by the Egyptians. Dreams considered positive took pride of place, with dreams considered negative listed after them, in red (red being a color which signified bad omens of destructive events being foretold, in the culture of the ancient Egyptians).

Over one hundred types of dreams are listed in the Egyptian Book of Dreams, most of them describing dreams which involved sight, or seeing things. Others describes dreams which involve food. There are also descriptions and interpretations of dreams in which sex is involved, as well as being given gifts, or receiving guests and family. All dreams listed describe scenes common to all people, for in daily life, the Egyptians saw more than the mundane. They saw that life's most apparently regular activities held within them the mysteries of dreams. They understood the subconscious as having a divine function; that of communication from the other, unseen side of the ordinary world.

The Egyptians of Rameses II's day believed that by interpreting their dreams, they could make decisions as important as whether to go to war and also those concerning state affairs. They believed fervently that dreams were a means of curing a variety of illnesses. They further believed that some dreams were premonitions to be heeded carefully. Dream interpretation had a central place in the culture and was so respected that the Book of Dreams papyrus was handed down from generation to generation, in order to preserve and disseminate the knowledge it contained.

Because of this document, we know that the Egyptians feared at least some of the same things we do. For example, a commonality between those times and our own is dreaming about teeth falling out, or drowning. But one unique feature of ancient Egyptian beliefs about dreams was the role of homonyms (words that sound alike, but differ in meaning, for example "bear" and "bare"). To encounter a dream which featured symbols which were homonyms was considered a sign of impending or continuing good fortune. Another unique feature is the interpretation of dreams based on which Egyptian god the dreamer was most devoted too. For example, those who followed Seth were believed to anger quickly, so this characteristic would be factored into the overall dream interpretation, guided by other factors. The consideration of religious status or belief may even be the case today, concerning modern methods of interpreting dreams. Individuality continues to be a central consideration when analyzing the meaning of dreams.

The Greek philosopher, Aristotle, suggested in the Third Century BCE, that true wisdom was only attainable in the realm of sleep, as whispered to us in dreams. Aristotle believed that the freedom known by the human mind in sleep was the only entry point for pure wisdom, unadulterated by prejudice or cultural imperatives.

Through the Delphic Oracle, Aristotle's suggestion was a general cultural belief in Ancient Greece, with the Oracle's pronouncements influencing the conduct of government and social norms. This Oracle received wisdom and divine inspiration only in sleep and this guided the actions of the Senate and all aspects of Greek society, including family life, military actions and the development of the emerging middle eastern world. Both prophetic and prescriptive, the Greek approach to dream interpretation was to depend on it in order to perceive the best ways to live in order to be prosperous. Also, dream interpretation was called upon to look into the future and heavily influenced government decision-making in all matters.

The *Oneirocritica,* probably the most important book to have ever been written on the subject of dream interpretation, comes to us from Ancient Greece, a testament to the importance of dreams in the Greek society of those times. Written by Artemidorus (also known as Ephesius) in the 2nd Century CE, this magisterial work consisted of five volumes and is the basis of most of the modern world' dream dictionaries, which incorporate its semiotic structure. Together with the work of Freud and Jung, the *Oneirocritica* stands as one of the most important influences on dream interpretation to ever have been written.

Considered the founder of modern medicine and the person for whom the Hippocratic Oath (which guides the conduct of all physicians to this day) is named, Hippocrates looked to dreams as a way to discern the wellbeing of patients. Hippocrates is considered to be the first person in recorded history to understand dreams as a psycho-somatic (intellectual-physical) phenomenon and not of divine origin. Interestingly, Hippocrates also lived long before Artemidorus and died fourteen years before

Aristotle's birth. Yet he took this extraordinarily progressive stance on the subject of dreams.

Ancient Roman society derived much of what it believed about dreams from the overwhelming influence of the Greeks. Roman Emperor Augustus Caesar is said to been an enthusiastic believer in dream interpretation and believed strongly in the prophetic power of dreams. Under his rule, it was the law that anyone in the Empire who'd had a dream concerning its conduct or future, was compelled to share it publicly with other citizens. The Ancient Romans also brought forward Hippocrates' assertion that dreams were not messages from the gods, but arose from human passions and emotions.

It's undeniable that we see the most potent link between the ancient world's concepts concerning dreams and those of our own time. The influence of the Greeks through the Romans, however, is not alone in speaking to the modern understanding of dreams, their analysis and interpretation. Primitive and aboriginal cultures have strong traditions in this area. Of all of them, the interpretive traditions of the aboriginal peoples of the Americas have become most inextricably intermeshed with those which come down to use from the ancient world. Further, these have served in the schema of the great interpreters, Joseph Campbell and Carl Jung.

In First Nations (aboriginal) culture, dream interpretation is the province of the Shaman, or Medicine man/woman. It's interesting to note here, that some First Nations people appoint an inter-sex (of both, or neither gender, specifically) or two-spirit (homosexual) person to serve in this role. People who differed from the default sexuality were considered to have greater insight and enhanced vision.

Dreams were and continue to be a strong cultural tradition among aboriginal people, who believe (as is the case with other ancient cultures), that the veil between the waking and sleeping worlds is not only thin, but fluid. Aboriginal people further believe that dreams may be had in a waking state, which is pursued through the tradition of the vision quest. Today, this cultural practice continues to exist and is practiced communally. Vision questers isolate themselves in the wilderness, fasting from food and water. There, they seek visions to illuminate their path forward. The tradition of the sweat lodge is another means of seeking visions, with participants abstaining from culturally interpolated substances like alcohol prior to a sweat ceremony, and then remaining in the lodge until such time as they receive the desired vision or visions.

In some aboriginal cultures, vision questing is pursued under the influence of naturally-occurring psychotropic substances (peyote mushrooms is only one of the many used in such ceremonies in the Americas). In Carlos Castaneda's book *The Teachings of Don Juan*, he details his exploration of the method of vision questing among the Toltec people of Mexico and that culture's use of peyote for spiritual purposes. The book was the start of a series on his study of the shamanic teachings of a Yaqui aboriginal man named Don Juan Matus. In Peru, the famous Ayahuasca ceremony continues to be practiced, placing those who partake of this vine, boiled with other natural substances and then consumed, in a state which makes them more open to the reception of spiritual enlightenment.

An important facet of aboriginal dream culture, where ever it's found, is the concept that human begins are part of the natural world and that it speaks to them as a unique, but integral part of it. Vision questing, the use of natural substances to provoke dream states and the holistic view of waking/dreaming life, point to First Nations culture in the Americas as the originator of lucid dreaming. The unique naturalism of aboriginal dream culture has probably been one of the most important spiritual influences on the West's apprehension of this form of dreaming.

Pre-dating the advent of modern psychotherapy and psychology is Sir Thomas Browne, an English doctor and one of the most important prose writers of his time. In his essay, *On Dreams*, Browne writes: "Half our days we pass in the shadow of the earth; and the brother of death exacteth a third part of our lives." Here he refers, of course, to the one third of our lives we humans spend sleeping. Sir Thomas continues the Hippocratic tradition, via the Romans, with regard to the origins of our dreams. His contention was that dreams were a replaying of the events of the previous day, or manifestations of our waking obsessions. Of St. John Chrysostom, he writes "Who can therefore wonder that Chrysostom should dream of St.

Paul, who daily read his epistles". He intimates that Chrysostom's focus on the writings of St. Paul (which dominate the Christian Scriptures), dominated his dreams due to his daily reading of them. He goes on to state that "Pious persons, whose thoughts are daily busied about heaven, and the blessed state thereof, can hardly escape the nightly phantasms of it." Browne's rejection of the delivery of visions and messages by God and his stated preference for a psychological explanation, places him well before him time.

Since the early 20th Century, the modern disciplines of psychology and psychotherapy have sought to understand the origin of dreams and their interpretation, toward a greater understanding of the workings of our minds. Beginning with the Austrian psychotherapist, Sigmund Freud, the scientific examination of the reasons we dream and how dreams might be interpreted to gain insight into human psychological realities, has been a rich source of scientific exploration.

The first recognized theory of dreams was that of Sigmund Freud. The father of modern psychotherapy (which some call the "taking cure"), Freud's contributions to our understanding of the human mind are immeasurable and the couch where his subjects lay as they unburdened themselves to him, recognized all over the world as the birthplace of modern psychiatry. Freud is the "proto-shrink".

Dreams

Freud's 1899 book, *The Interpretation of Dreams*, introduced his theory that the human mind and motivations arising were at least partially attributable to a function which was unconscious, and entirely unknown to people as a source of their thoughts, actions and emotional states. The book served as the basis for the idea that the interpretation of our dreams might be helpful in the treatment of mental illness and dysfunction.

It wasn't until Freud published the third edition of the book that an extensive section on the symbolism of dreams was added, in which he attributed literal interpretations to the appearance of these symbols in dreams. This advent was the product of Freud's understanding of the work of Wilhelm Steckel, who was a contemporary and with Freud, one of the originators of modern psychoanalytic thought.

Freud posited that dreams functioned as a form of unconscious wish fulfillment, allowing the dreamer to continue sleeping peacefully, as his subconscious sent the message that all was well, due to the fulfilment of existing hopes and desires. He suggested that they did this, yy playing out latent (unexpressed) desires in the realm of dreams and disguising these through "dream work" with symbolic surrogates (which Freud called "manifest content").

Freud believed he could discover what was at the bottom of the mental disturbances and dysfunction being experienced by those on his couch through a process of free association. This process sought to uncover what came to the mind of the patient when dream symbol were described to him by patients. What Freud sought was not necessarily the patient's response to the symbol itself, but rather the emotions experienced by the patient when considering the symbol's role in the context of the dream under examination. The patient's response, Freud believed, held the key to the latent content of the dream, hidden under the manifestation of its symbolic content. This key, he further believed, had the potential to mitigate neurosis and similar dysfunction in his patients.

You may remember I wrote earlier that "sometimes a cigar is just a cigar". Freud is the person who is purported to have originally said this and in saying it, he acknowledged that all apparent symbols present in dreams don't necessarily have a specific meaning, or any meaning at all. Sometimes pink poodles, talking parrots, or floating politicians disguised as wolves, are nothing more significant than the day's detritus having a dream time curtain call. Sometimes, though, a cigar is the manifest content/symbol of a dream which points to a latent desire, problem, or fear. I don't suppose it's necessary I elaborate on Freud's take on the symbolic meaning of a cigar in dreams, as he was famous for his psychoanalytic work in the area of human sexuality.

Sigmund Freud was soon to be followed by one of the foremost proponents of dream analysis, Carl Jung. An ardent student and follower of Freud, Jung forged a new direction in the field. Jung saw the world of dreams, rooted as they are in the work of the subconscious, as having a primarily spiritual basis. It's not surprising that Freud and Jung were to go their separate ways over their divergent understanding of the role of dreaming.

Jung's assertion was that dreams were not so much the subconscious mind's attempt to conceal latent desires, but rather, to create a communicative link between the conscious and unconscious parts of the mind. By creating this link, the conscious mind could be illuminated by the subconscious, leading us to greater insights about ourselves and the world around us. Jung also believed that we all have within us a "counter ego", which stands in silent opposition to our "ego", which is the way in which we want others to see us. Jung referred to this counter ego as "the shadow" – rather like an evil twin of ourselves we'd rather the world didn't know about. This is our least favorite version of ourselves, but the one we fear may be the whole truth. It's also the part of ourselves we choose not to reveal to others, but fear may be uncovered, causing us to be despised as others realize who we truly are. Jung believed that what we reject about ourselves are those aspects most in need of bringing into the light, in order to fully know and mitigate.

He also believed that dreams are revelatory, straightforward expressions of our creative impulse, offering us a self-generated mythology about our subconscious that serves as a form of silent narrative. This personal mythology, Jung believed, could be drawn upon to know ourselves more fully. It's important to note here that Jung didn't believe the interpretation of dreams was necessary for them to build the interpretative bridge between our subconscious and conscious minds. Rather, he posited that this bridge was still being built because of a process he called individuation. This concept was to form the basis for analytical psychology, and referred to the process of reconciling the tensions between opposites (subconscious/conscious, for one).

Jung was also responsible for developing the psychological concept of the archetype. This particular facet of Jung's thinking is highly relevant to the subject of dream interpretation. Archetypes, are images and patterns drawn from what he called "the collective unconscious" – an underlying, communal recognition of the meaning of universal symbols and experiences. His archetypes are a close parallel to universal dream symbols and heavily influenced the modern understanding on these, as indications of psychological realities and meta-cultural symbols we all share (the flood, mother and the child, among them). The universality of archetypes, through the subconscious mind, is processed by the individual into interpretations of the deepest part of the self, in Jung's model. This is very near to the ideas we will discuss later, concerning the importance of individual and cultural interpretations of universal dream symbols. Jung further believed that his archetypal hypothesis represented the psychological counterpart of "instinct", which is rooted in the primitive brain and our physical responses to its promptings (fight or flight, for example).

Calvin Spring Hall Jr. was an avid student of both Freud and Jung and further developed the field of dream interpretation, which he began studying and researching in the 1940s, in the United States. Hall took a systematic approach to his research, examining statistics gathered from thousands of study participants to arrive at his theory of dreams, which was his cognitive theory, emerging in 1953. Its emergence was the result of Hall's extensive, systematic research.

Our ideas of ourselves and who we are were central to Hall's theory. Extending from that basis, our way of seeing the world around us, including our friends, family and cultural context, as well as our social milieu, is reflected in our dreams. The subconscious undermines, in dreams, the self we show the world (which closely follows Freud's idea of the role of dreaming). We often wear masks in public, insisting that the world around us know us in the way we wish we could truly be. The authentic self is more fully experienced in the subconscious, through our dreams. While we're awake, we fool not only the world, but ourselves. While we're asleep, on the other hand, there's no escape from ourselves, as the subconscious reveals what's underneath the masks we wear. Latent dream content (what's behind the symbols) helps us understand our most primal fears and anxieties. Manifest dream content, in Hall's model, stands in for our distorted self-conceptions and emotions. He also believed that these two aspects of dream content implied that dreams had more than one meaning – the meaning we want to believe and the meaning we *should*, by rights, believe (as revelatory of the self).

Joseph Campbell's work as a mythologist is best known in the phrase "follow your bliss". His study, research and writing in the field of comparative religions and mythology has deeply influenced popular culture's understanding of universal human culture and the role of our dreams in our lives. Campbell is best remembered for the PBS television series he made with Bill Moyers – The Power of Myth. The series was an in depth exploration of mythology and psychological archetypes (following Jung's ideas about these) and led to a popular resurgence of interest in these subjects.

While not engaged, per se, in the active study of dream interpretation, Campbell's contribution lies in his association of the spiritual with the psychological and how this association is extant in all spiritual systems. He believed that the idea of "following your bliss" was the pursuit of one's highest calling and the result of an active decision on the part of the person following personal bliss to know the deepest self. That knowledge could arise from examining archetypal representations in mythological and religious narratives, which he believed to be universal. Saying that "myths allow us to enter into a holy picture", it was Campbell's belief that myths operated on multiple levels which revealed core truths about the nature of being human. Jung "personal mythology" flows through time to become part of Campbell's semiotic and mythological world. Campbell forwarded the idea of "mythos as personal revelation", which is a direct descendent of Jungian thinking on the subject of myth.

As the history of dream interpretation, from ancient Mesopotamia to Joseph Campbell reveals, all dream theorists see the role of dreams in our lives as offering potential solutions to our problems and challenges. They believe dreams occur when we're facing problems in life we're at an impasse in resolving, or seeking to heal an old hurt, or soothe a current anxiety, or psychological reality in need of treatment. The common theme in the field's history is that dreams tell us something important about ourselves. While Jung didn't believe that dream interpretation was necessary for dreams to create a link between our subconscious and conscious minds, he nonetheless believe they served an important psychological purpose. In his case, that purpose was to build a bridge between these two psychic realities. In Freud's case, it was to reveal what was being hidden from the waking self (as in Hill's) in order to reconcile the whole. Clearly, what the modern, psychologically-based system of dream interpretation hopes to do is to bring integrity to the human psyche, even though the roads to that integrity are expressed somewhat differently.

While the ancients believed that dreams were messages from the gods, our modern Shamans believe they are messages from the deepest part of ourselves. Campbell's mythology, via Jung's personal mythology of archetypes (universal patterns and images) arrives at a modern synthesis of the spiritual with the psychological, which brings us to an understanding of the world of dreams as the place in which our spirits and psyches meet.

The psychological interpretation of dreams is now a modern, integrative discipline which takes into account the whole person, revealing deep-seated truths about ourselves only accessible when we take a journey over the bridge from our subconscious to our conscious minds. A human reality for 5,000 years, dream interpretation still enjoys a vibrant place in our lives. In the modern, technocratic age, we are increasingly being called on to abandon the emotional aspect of our natures in favor of a mechanistic vision of what the human animal is. For this reason, dreams tend not to be taken seriously by many and thus, written off as psycho-babble. Their often strange, mysterious nature causes our logic-driven age to dismiss them as psychic detritus of little value in our waking lives. Operating in highly imaginative and sometimes distorted ways, their mystery and mythology is a rich field of self-revelation in the modern age; a personal theatre of the soul and subconscious. While it's easy to pass them off as nonsensical entertainment for our sleeping brains, the truth is that our fascination with them over the ages points to a central function in our lives we can't ignore.

Sometimes we encounter dreams that wake us up in the middle of the night and affect us so deeply we can't shake them. Dreams like that, resonating at the very core of our beings, can change the course of our lives and sometimes even history (as we'll see shortly). Dreams like this are regarded in native cultures as messages from a higher consciousness or the spirit world of the ancestors. Regardless of what you may believe their source to be, these profound dreams often having life-changing impacts on the dreamer and the dreamer's community. In many cultures, people who have such dreams are thought of prophets, or oracles.

As we've learned in our walk through the history of dream interpretation, many ancient cultures assigned a special position in their communities to those able to interpret dreams and to further instruct the dreamer on what course of action to take in order to fully realize the dream's message.

These types of dreams not as rare as you may think. In the Bible, dreams serve many purposes, including that of etiology and that's because most of us dream and many of us have dreams which have worked to help us understand our life's purpose and direction. Prophetic dreams usually come to those who have a very high purpose in life. Dreams like these make no distinction as to what the cultural background of the dreamer is, validating the notion that certain types of dreams are common to all humans. Our dreams and visions and seeking to understand them, can help us focus more clearly on our purpose in life. Consider the impact Martin Luther King Jr. had on the United States of America in his speech on the Washington Mall, in 1963, which spoke of his dream for America. It may surprise some of you to know that, in speaking of his dream, he called on an ancient text in the Christian Scriptures:

"I have a dream that one day every valley shall be exalted, and every hill and mountain shall be made low, the rough places will be made plain, and the crooked places will be made straight; "and the glory of the Lord shall be revealed and all flesh shall see it together."

Here, Dr. King alludes to the story of John the Baptist and his mission to prepare the way for the coming of Jesus of Nazareth's ministry. The mission of the Baptist is brought forward to the contemporary political situation Dr. King was addressing – racial segregation and the Jim Crow laws. In invoking the Baptist, his message calls upon those listening to enter into the mission of bringing justice; making straight the ways for its immediate passage. Lowered mountains and exalted valleys speak to the need for equality, as the playing field of America is levelled. In calling on the ancient text, Dr. King frames the Civil Rights struggle as one of epic, Biblical proportions and portrays the justice of legislated equality as a modern incarnation of God.

But this historic figure (who was a minister) drew on Biblical imagery as collective archetypes throughout his career as the leader of the Black liberation movement in the United States. In the text of the final speech he was ever to give (on April 3, 1968, in Memphis, Tennessee) he speaks of another dream, that of Moses:

"And I've seen the Promised Land. I may not get there with you. But I want you to know tonight, that we, as a people, will get to the promised land!"

These words, spoken on the night before his assassination on the balcony of the Loraine Motel, seem to express a premonition on Dr. King's part that he would not live to see the promised land, himself. Like Moses, who was shown the promised land by God and told that he would be "gathered unto his people" (die) (Numbers 27:13), before he would enter it, Dr. King knew he would not get there with his people. Like Moses, he would only glimpse it from the mountaintop.

The Bible, as a blend of Hebrew culture with those of the people the ancient Hebrews lived among in the ancient near east, is a rich source of dream history and symbolism. As you've seen above, Dr. King drew on it heavily, reinterpreting its motifs to apply to his day and illuminate the struggles of American Blacks by juxtaposing them against those of the Hebrew people, captive in hostile Egypt. His evocation of the theme of Egypt echoes that of Black American slaves, only permitted to learn something of the Bible and no other book. In their abusive captivity, they came to see themselves and their story reflected in the story of the Hebrew slaves, captive in Israel. As ancient books go, those of the Bible can illuminate contemporary life in many ways and the role of dreams in our lives is no exception.

Let's take a walk through the pages of the Bible and explore some of the famous dreams and visions that populate its ancient pages.

The dream life of the Bible

Whether you cleave to the collected books of the Bible as Holy Writ, works of literature, or just ancient attempts at figuring out why we're all here, it's a collection of fascinating insights into the world the writers lived it. Produced over the space of more than a millennium, these books were transmitted orally before being written down. History confirms that they have been subjected to interpretation by the many cultures who've explored and believed in their contents as Salvation History, up to the present day.

As the literature of ancient peoples, these books are cultural artifacts of a 1,400 year time span and include the contribution of no fewer than forty writers. Their gift to the modern age is that they illuminate that time period from a cultural and religious perspective, as well as revealing the type of world they were produced in, over time. What's abundantly clear, in studying the historical context of the Bible's books, is that the ancient near east was a vibrant melting pot of cultures, interchanging traditions, religious practices and languages freely.

As I've noted early, the Gilgamesh Epic is a striking example of Babylonian literature entering the canon of scripture, in the flood narrative. The exchange of content and ideas was extremely fluid in these times. One idea that was universal in the ancient near east, though, was

23

that of the interpretation of dreams and the divine origin of the messages they brought to ancient dreamers from the Creator.

Following are some of the most vibrant examples of dreams in the Bible and how they were interpreted by those who wrote about them, as expositions of God's living presence in the midst of the people.

Great Dreamers of the Bible

The Bible, throughout the Hebrew and Christian Scriptures is replete with descriptions of dreams. In every instance, these are messages from God and many are premonitions of things to come. Let's look at several examples and the symbolism that appears in them.

Pharaoh's Dreams – Genesis 41: 1-7

During the captivity of the Hebrews in Egypt, an unnamed Pharaoh has two dreams. In the first he sees seven fat healthy cows while standing on the banks of the Nile. These are followed by seven, unhealthy, skinny, diseased cows who consume the fat cows before his eyes.

As many of us do, Pharaoh woke up following this disturbing dream, questioning it's meaning. Finally, he falls asleep and dreams a second time. The subsequent dream follows the plot of the first, with the healthy and unhealthy cows replaced by seven healthy heads of grain and seven unhealthy ones. Again, the healthy stock is consumed by the unhealthy stock.

What was Pharaoh to make of all this? We needn't wonder, as Pharaoh's dreams are interpreted right in the narrative by none other than Joseph (the guy with the coat of many colors). Pharaoh's cupbearer, on hearing of Pharaoh's disturbing dreams suggests to him that Joseph be called to interpret them, as it's known among the royal staff that he's able to do this. Even though Joseph has said at an earlier point in the narrative that dream interpretation belongs to God (Gen. 40:8), what he meant by this is that interpretation is to be appointed to an intermediary. Joseph will no doubt have absorbed the Egyptian approach to dream interpretation during his time at Pharaoh's court. His gift, having been recognized by others, was to elevate to him to some stature in the complex royal hierarchy.

So Joseph is summoned and ritually prepared to act as an interpreter, by being bathed and shaved (Gen. 41: 14). This ritual preparation, it should be noted, points to the importance of dream interpretation in the Egyptian society of the time, as noted in the section on the Egyptian Book of Dreams. Identified practitioners were expected to prepare themselves physically for the act of interpretation.

Pharaoh then recounts to Joseph, now invested as a court dream interpreter, the manifest content of his dreams. Upon hearing and considering them, Joseph tells Pharaoh things he most probably doesn't care to hear, because his interpretation is bleak. He tells Pharaoh that the dream is a message warning of seven years of plenty, follow by a further seven of famine. He then tells him that the two dreams, when considered together, point to the rapid onset of famine and an unknown event horizon. Joseph therefore counsels Pharaoh to set aside a proportion of the crops of the plentiful years in order to survive the impending years of famine. This one act of interpretation serves to elevate his situation in Pharaoh's royal court.

Ezekiel in the Valley of Dry Bones (Ezekiel 37: 1-10)

Some of you may only know this tale from the old song "Dem Bones", but this American spiritual tells the story of a dream in which God commands Ezekiel to act as his servant and bring an entire nation back to him.

Ezekiel's dream begins with a visit from God, in which his body is transported to a valley. The vision in his dream points to a physical projection, along the lines of what some claim is astral projection (leaving the body, or travelling to a remote location while in one's body, while dreaming).

In the valley, God tells Ezekiel to observe the bones on the valley floor. He then commands that Ezekiel speak to the bones, telling them that God is commanding that they reconstitute themselves as the human beings they were before they came to be dried out bones, littering the ground. He says that Ezekiel must speak them into life, ordering them to take on flesh, sinew and tendon.

As Ezekiel looks on, the bones begin to rattle and reconstitute as human forms, but are not fully animated, as they lack humanity's central component – the breath of God that animated the mud doll in the Creation Narrative. God then commands Ezekiel to bid the four winds to come and breath into the dead the breath of life. The now enfleshed, animated human beings then stand before Ezekiel as a host, ready for action.

In exegetical terms (those which govern the interpretation of scripture by comparing passages which illuminate each other), God has brought Ezekiel to the bone-littered valley in order to impress upon him the importance of a renaissance to the people of Israel. The dry bones are theirs. Their hope and will to continue having been exhausted, they have forgotten who they are and so God puts human flesh on them. It's not until the *"ruach"* (the breath of God) is put in them, though, that they remember themselves to be the people of Israel. Dryness in this narrative refers to spiritual aridity or estrangement from the God who created the Hebrew community to be mystical "Israel", to begin with. The narrative, in calling on "breath", or "wind" harkens back to the mud doll narrative of the Creation narrative in the book of Genesis and humanity's intimacy with God, through that breath.

God's commission to Ezekiel, to maintain the foundation of the nation of Israel in leading it back to the service of

God, reconstitutes the community in the rosy life humanity knew at the dawn of humanity's Creation. Ezekiel's dream equates the dryness of human bones in an arid valley with a lack of spiritual tenacity. By reaching back into scripture to the original creation narrative, the dream reminds us that humanity is animated by the breath of God, thus sharing in the divine mission for Creation, as its stewards and caretakers.

Joseph's dreams (Matthew 1 and 2) and The Annunciation to Mary (Luke 1:26-38)

There is a rich complex of dreams around the birth of Jesus of Nazareth. These dreams are characterized by angelic visitations in the case of both Joseph (who is visited on four occasions in the Gospel of Matthew) and Mary (who is visited by Gabriel in the Gospel of Luke, and brought the good news that she will bear the Holy Child).

While these dreams are solidly within the Hebrew tradition of prophetic and revelatory dreams, their having been written down well after the events they described occurred, have had the effect of historicizing the original prophecy. In so doing, they build a historical foundation to support the attendant theological assertions, which were not to fully emerge until the 4th Century, concerning the person of Jesus and its religious significance. Prophecy historicized takes on the gloss of the emerging Christian religion, re-telling a tale transmitted orally for generations, prior to being written down and eventually entering the canon of scripture, as we know it today. Regardless, these accounts stand as examples of dreams in the Christian Scripture which carry Hebrew tradition forward into Early Christianity, particularly the tradition of angelic visitation, as originally derived from Sumerian mythology.

In Matthew 1: 20-21, Joseph's angelic visit is for the purpose of advising him to take Mary as his wife. He's also told that she has conceived a child and that he is to be named "Yeshuah" (YHWH – God is salvation) and that the child will save humanity from its sins. The use of the tetragrammaton (YHWH) in relation to the naming of Jesus and its deliberate transliteration represents a departure from Hebrew tradition. While the name is a common one in the Hebrew tradition, the angel's use of it in this passage is the root of Christian soteriology (salvation theology) around the person of Jesus, as the *hoi anthropos* (human one), who brings with him salvation from sin, as the incarnation (enfleshment) of God. While considering this passage, it's interesting to remember what we read about Ezekiel in the valley of dry bones and his dream of those bones becoming enfleshed and then animated by the breath of God. Similarly, the angel's message to Joseph speaks of the enfleshment of God in a child to be born to Mary.

In Joseph's second dream (Matt. 2:22), he's told to take his wife (now heavy with child) and flee to Egypt, effectively making them refugees from the land of Israel. In telling Joseph to take the family to Egypt to escape Herod's slaughter, the message is clearly that the land in which the Hebrews were once enslaved will now serve God's purpose by protecting the life of the Holy Child, come to save humanity from its sins. Egypt's appearance in this narrative is more than just a geographical accident (as a neighboring state). In the Hebrew Scriptural tradition, Egypt stands as an icon of captivity and slavery. The symbolism of Egypt in Joseph's dream reveals it as powerless against the coming salvation enfleshed in the child to be born to Mary.

In the third dream visitation (Matt. 2:19-20), occurring while the family is in Egypt, Joseph is urged to return to Israel, as the coast is now clear. Herod, once a threat to the survival of the Holy Child has died. Herod's death, in this dream, represents the death of Imperial power over the people of Judaea. As Caesar's vassal overlord, Herod served the interests of Rome. His death, in this narrative, clears the way for a new order for the people of Israel - one ruled by God as enfleshed in the salvific person of Christ. Again, it's no accident that death takes Herod at this time and that the family is in Egypt when news of his death arrives. Having entered the lands of Egypt, once the source of Hebrew suffering and slavery, the Holy Family emerges from the adventure unscathed. Returning to post-Herodian Israel, the symbolism of victory over worldly imperialism and slavery is doubly reinforced in the dream.

But the family of Joseph is still not out of the woods. In his fourth dream, he's told that Herod's son has taken the reins of Roman-occupied Judaea and decides to strike out for rural Galillee, not knowing the disposition of the new vassal and fearing he might be as brutal as his dead father. But it's his choice of city which is most interesting in this account. Bethlehem translates from the Hebrew as "house of bread". Jesus is referred to in the Gospel of John (written much later) as the "bread of life" (John 6:35). What's most interesting about Bethlehem, though, is that it is the city of King David (of whose house, Joseph is also a member) which brings us to the Annunciation of Mary.

In Mary's angelic dream visitation, the angel tells her she is to give birth to the "son of God" and calls her blessed for having been chosen expressly for the honor. Mary, though, litigates with the angel, asking how it is she's conceived without "knowing a man". The angel explains that God will "overshadow her", in order for the conception to occur.

The idea of virgin births exists in the Hebrew Scriptures, most strikingly, in the lineage of Jesus. It's no coincidence that his Davidic lineage includes such notables as Sarah, Rebecca and Rachel, all the recipients of miraculous births. But in relation to the Annunciation Dream, a direct, exegetical parallel is that of the birth of Immanuel, in Isaiah 7:14. Readers with recognize this name in relation to Jesus as one of the names he's known by in the Christian tradition, particularly manifested in the Christmas hymn "O Come, O Come, Immanuel". The name itself means "God with us" and appears in Matt. 1: 23 with reference to Jesus as the incarnation God, born of a virgin.

The narrative in Isaiah provides an exegetical support for the identification of Jesus as the Messiah, but does not refer to original Immanuel in Messianic terms, even though the name, in the Gospel of Matthew is directly called upon in conferring that status. Rather, the name refers to another birth (not miraculous, but offered by God as a sign in the conduct of a contemporary war), most probably that of the prophet Hezekiah. The prophet Isaiah relates to King Ahaz that a woman will bear a son, with the news standing as a good omen with respect to Israel's position in the war with Syria at that time.

Miraculous, or divinely-generated birth, was a popular theme in other ancient near eastern cultures, as well. The most striking example is that of the Egyptian goddess, Isis. The ancient Egyptians believed in *parthenogenesis* (conception without sexual intercourse), specifically among the gods and goddesses. They believed, from the earliest layer of their recorded history, that the god Horus had been conceived via divine means to be born to Isis. This tradition stems from the goddess, Net, who was said to be the origin of all life, existing before time began. Serving as the Creator of all in Egyptian mythology, Net is Egypt's mythological answer to the masculine conception of God in the Judeo-Christian complex of belief. What's of great interest here is that the angel's visitation casts Mary in a very similar role and yet, she refers to herself as "handmaid of the Lord", choosing a humbler role for herself than that of the Egyptian, Net.

Again, it's important to note that the dream's symbolism has been heavily influenced by later translations, glosses and redactions. From the original narrative, transmitted orally, has come this account, replete with imagery that stems from both Hebrew and Egyptian sources and the syncretic (religious meshing, or the absorption of beliefs and traditions from surrounding religious groups) relationship between the two belief systems. Later scribes were to have their way with the text in order to ensure that its content conformed to the theology of the emerging church and even later, to beliefs that had become concretized through time.

Clearly, dreams and their interpretation was a matter of extreme importance in the ancient near east, as played out on the pages of the Bible. The presence of angels in many of them, similarly bears witness to the many cultural strands which influenced the Bible, due to the Sumerian origin of the concept of angels as emissaries of the Creator. The complex interpretation and exegetical complexity of the texts cited is a rich source of interest for anyone interested in the history of dream interpretation. The Bible is filled with such accounts and despite its reputation as a fusty old rule book, it offers the alert and engaged reader a glimpse into the dream world of the ancients and a fascinating background for modern, would be dream interpreters.

Dreams in motion pictures

Motion pictures are the waking land of dreams for millions of movie goers around the world. Their wide spread diffusion in the early 20th Century coincided with some of the most difficult times the United States of America had ever known, providing average people with a means of escape from their economically-depressed lives.

In the darkness of the movie theater, people found a way to forget about the world outside, entering into the make believe of the Wild West, villains tying helpless heroines to the railroad tracks and the glitz of high society. But motion pictures also have a strong thematic tendency to manifest the unseen, including the unseen land of dreams. Today, they represent a means of escape for people all over the world.

A Christmas Carol

Who can forget the dreams of Scrooge, in *A Christmas Carol*, the cinematic adaptation of Charles Dickens' timeless Victorian-era novel? His dreams display, for his edification, his life, past, present and future, through three specters representing the Christmases of his life. He is shown, through their agency, the cost of his miserliness, in the impact it has on the lives of those around him, ultimately leading to a radical shift in his attitude to life. Scrooge comes to an understanding of the error of his ways, choosing a better kind of life, because of the message of the Christmas specters. Dickens' classic illustrates the power of dreaming as a means of self-examination and a personal dedication to the betterment of one's ethical framework.

American Beauty

In the film *American Beauty*, the middle-aged protagonist, Lester, becomes obsessed with a teenaged cheerleader. His obsession leads him to have a dream in which rose petals fall over him, referencing the film's title (American Beauty is a variety of the rose flower). Beginning with a single petal wafting down to land on his prone figure, Lester is soon covered in rose petals as he gazes upward, ecstatic and transported by this dream, fueled by his sexual fantasies. In bed next to his sleeping wife, the source of his ecstasy is the cheerleader, who lies on the ceiling on a bed of rose petals, strategically and scantly covered by them, as she gazes back. The scene is reminiscent of an early, classic photograph of Marilyn Monroe, the ultimate icon of the American blonde. Symbolic of love and beauty, the rose is also considered to be a symbol of the male phallus in the interpretation of dreams. Appearing as petals, the reference may be to female power over male sexuality; emasculating the whole into fragments of the no-longer-potent phallus, which has disintegrated in the face of youthful womanhood.

Time of the Gypsies

The cult film, *Time of the Gypsies*, by director Emir Kusturica, is the story of a family of Roma people in

Eastern Europe and the teenaged boy, Perhan, who is invested with mystical telekinetic gifts. Perhan's fortunes change dramatically when he goes on a journey of discovery, misery, love and loss which illustrates the oppression and resilience of the Roma people. The film seems almost like a dream itself, with its hypnotic music, surreal characters and settings and lavish dream sequences.

One of these is staged during the most important day of the Roma calendar, Ederlezi (the rites of Spring). To heighten the ethereal scene, in which candles float on the waters of a slow running river and people wade into the river to ritually cleanse themselves, the traditional song plays. The quality of the woman singer's voice transports the viewer into the world of the dream, its languid, mystery seemingly brought to life in the music. The film's protagonist, Perhan, is pictured floating above the scene, cradling his pet turkey, as he gazes down on the scene. As the dream proceeds, Perhan is confronted by his love, a girl from the village, standing topless in the water.

The pair floats downstream in a small boat, as Perhan's grandmother watches from the shore, observing the transition of her son into manhood. Perhan is next seen standing in the water again, as his love wades toward the shore, now fully clothed. He watches her go wistfully, as we again see his grandmother wiping a tear from her face in the realization that he's now a man and no longer a boy. The Rites of Spring in Roma culture employ fertility symbols which have existed since the dawn of time, including the cracking of decorated eggs on people's heads, as a symbolic blessing for an abundant season in terms of both agricultural production and human fertility. Against this backdrop, Perhan's transition to virile manhood signals a profound rite of passage and the loss of the child to the man, as well as the impending mortality of the grandmother.

Because of the miracle of film, we are now able to see filmic depictions of dreams as symbolic art. Freud and Jung would have been enthralled to see their theories so eloquently made real in moving pictures. In the case of *A Christmas Carol*, the dream sequences serve a distinctly moral and expository purpose. The specters are surrogates for Scrooge's better angels, speaking from his subconscious to his decidedly unpleasant conscious. *American Beauty* tells the classic tale of male mid-life crisis and the power of femininity to provoke it to its most damaging levels. The symbolism in the rose petal dream, encompassing love, beauty and male emasculation, is baldly psychological and a classic of the dream sequence device in modern film. In the case of *Time of the Gypsies*, Kusturica evokes the mysticism of Roma culture, using the great Roma hymn to Spring, "Ederlezi" to set the mood of the dream sequence on the river. As with our own dreams, there's a quality of awe, even though what's depicted is a common human activity – a celebration marking the passage of time. The motif of transition via sexuality and the life cycle turning is powerful and universal.

Cinema's contribution to the interpretation and recognition of the importance of our dreams is undeniably powerful. Because of its role as a central, communal means of escape from the ordinary world (sometimes depicting scenes which are uniquely ordinary, yet heightened on the big screen), the powerful medium of cinema provides an artistic window for the apprehension of meaning human beings have always pursued in seeking to understand their dreams. The influence of film on the popular resurgence of interest in the field of dream interpretation is a kind of reference, inviting people to see their inner world through new eyes, coming to a better understanding of themselves and the world they live in. Cinema represents, for this reason, a type of renaissance whose art, in imitating life, invites us to imitate art, in turn.

Dreamers in history

The tradition of dream interpretation forms a unique area in the world's recorded history. We've reviewed some of the ancient world's traditions, including those extant in the canon of the Hebrew and Christian Scriptures, but history is replete with examples of its leaders and protagonists encountering dreams which changed its course by influencing the decisions of those who made it.

Socrates and the Phaedo

The great Greek philosopher, Socrates, spent his final days writing a series of treatises chronicling what he knew was to be the end of his life and discussing the nature of what lay beyond. The Phaedo is the final installment and is also known as *"On the Soul"*.

Socrates was something of a rebel in his times, challenging the existing religious order of gods and encouraging free thought, particularly among young people. Condemned to execution (which took the form of forced suicide in Greek society), by hemlock, Socrates faces death by doing what he does best - philosophizing. The volume is named after one of Socrates' most devoted students, Phaedo, who was at the philosopher's side at the time of his death. Also responsible for recording Socrates' thoughts at the time of his impending execution, he is said to have related these to Echecrates, the Pythagorean, resulting in one of Plato's most famous works. The book takes the form of discussion between the friends of Socrates, as they attend on the day of his death to discuss the nature of immortality and the afterlife.

Central to the Phaedo are Socrates' dreams. While awaiting his imminent execution, the philosopher had been writing poetry, the reason being that he was keen to explore the nature of his dreams and their relationship to the afterlife and its unseen world. He'd been experiencing recurring dreams of which he wrote "...frequently the same dream came to me, appearing at different times in different visages". His words reveal that while the recurring dream followed a basic plotline, its manifest content would change from dream to dream, in terms of who was in it. Repeatedly these "visages" would exhort Socrates to "make music", and so, hoping to appease the dreams (and perhaps banish them, due to their recurring nature), he wrote poetry in obedience to their exhortations.

Socrates then set his poems to music, fashioning them into hymns to the god, Apollo (strangely, in diametric defiance of the charges put against him by the Athenian court). He also set the fables of Aesop to music, during this time. In so doing, he follows the Greek idea that dreams must be "tested" to discern whether they're "friendly" or "hostile". Deeming the dreams friendly, Socrates believes that in doing philosophy he's already making a kind of music, but hedges his bets, nonetheless. To the Greeks, dream interpretation was a very serious business, involving obedience to any given dream's prompting in order to appease, banish, or manifest the lessons they led the dreamer toward.

In this respect, Socrates' dreams follow the philosophical impulse. While some feature visual content, of particular interest to the philosopher was the directive in the dream. In fact, Socrates saw all the dreams he had at this time as a unity, representing a sole imperative, which was to continue in his life's work (philosophy) even unto death. His response to the dream was to pass its contents on to others to memorialize in the literature of his day. This comes down to us as a vibrant record which forms the basis for Western thought, including much of what we have tried to apprehend about the afterlife and the possibility of an immortal soul.

Emperor Constantine I

On October 28, in 312 CE, two competing Roman Emperors faced each other on the Milvian bridge, an important trade conduit for the Imperial City of Rome. In the end, Constantine prevailed, becoming the sole Emperor. As for competing claimant, Maxentius, he ended up in the depths of the mighty Tiber, both vanquish and drowned.

On the night before the battle, Constantine was to have a glorious vision. The story is recounted by his historian, Eusebius of Caesarea, later to become a noted author, exegete and bishop (only two years after the Milvian Bridge battle). Eusebius writes that Constantine saw a vision of the Christian God, telling him to compel his soldiers to mark their shields with the "Chi-Ro" (the first two letters of the word Christ), saying, "In this sign, you will conquer". Constantine and his company followed the instruction and were, in fact, victorious. According to Eusebius, the incident marked the moment of Constantine's conversion to the Christian faith and led to the Edict of Milan (also called the Edict of Toleration), which made the practice of the Christian Faith legal in the Roman Empire, after centuries of marginalization in its Pagan context.

Somewhat contrary to this assertion is that the Arch of Constantine (which continues to stand in Rome, as the Milvian Bridge does) bears no overt Christian symbolism, while acknowledging the role of Constantine's dream in the victory. It's also notable that the currency of the Roman Empire, under Constantine's rule, continued to feature the image of Sol Invictus (the sun god) on its coinage. All the same, the long term result of Constantine's dream was the eventual creation of Christianity as the state religion (under Emperor Theodosius, in 380 CE) and the decline of Paganism.

Oliver Cromwell

Cromwell is best remembered as the political force responsible for overthrowing the English monarchy and creating of England a Commonwealth. For his efforts, he became Lord Protector of England and arguably one of the most powerful figures in English history.

As a young man, Cromwell experienced a dream he was not to fully understand until much later in his life. In the dream, an enormous woman arrives next to his bed, and pulls back the drapery surrounding it. The towering figure then declares that he will grow up to become the greatest man in the country. The following morning, Cromwell awoke to wonder what the dream had meant. He was of the belief, at the time, that the most powerful man in the nation was the King and none other. Being a commoner and not of noble birth, it was well beyond his imagination how it was he might rise to know such stature.

Cromwell went on to the be the man who signed the death warrant of Charles I, a very powerful act, indeed. It was only at that this time he was to gain insight in the dream he'd had in his youth. The towering figure of the woman was England, herself (often represented as mother of her people). The pulling back of the draperies on his bed represents a revelation of the future. Cromwell's dream is thus a striking example of an historical dream as a premonition which came to be reality, in all its historical fullness.

Edwin Moses

Edwin Moses went to the 1983 Olympic Games as a 400 meter hurdler. Having set a record for the event in 1980, he was a favorite to win again. What's extraordinary about his eventual win is what he later recounted concerning a recurring dream he'd had prior to the day of his record-breaking win.

In his dreams, Moses saw two sets of numbers, repeatedly. These were 47.03 and his birthday – 8-31-83. Interestingly the date of the race he was to win was also that of his birthday. As to the other numbers, these would have represented an excellent (and record-breaking) time for the race he was to run in. As it happened, Edwin Moses won the race at 47.02. While not the same number as the one in his recurring dream, the time was close enough to be rather alarming to him. It was only 1/10th of a second off the time seen in his dream. That razor sharp margin is also why his time in 1983 beat the record he'd established in 1980 by 1/10th of a second.

The story of Edwin Moses is yet another example of dreams bearing messages to us about the future – ones we can't easily explain.

Why do we dream?

Freud once claimed that every person is a poet, whether or not he intended to be one. He stated this is because we dream. He believed that dreams are very much like poetry. It's instructive to note that Socrates, apparently, agreed with him, as seen in the section on his dream as detailed in the Phaedo of Plato. A poet expresses the glories of life and its experiences through poetry; through his or her thoughts, joys, and sorrows, and an intricate tapestry of life experience is created. Dreams are the backroom workstation. In dreams, we create images and combine those images with the various elements which give rise to our emotional responses. Dreams are the stories that run through our unconscious minds, and these stories are based on everything but logic.

We live our lives being told stories as well as telling ourselves and others stories. Our personal history is a story. Our insights and experiences are stories. The more we tell ourselves the same story, the more we believe in it and act to make it true, manifesting our personal mythologies. Our stories can hold us back by causing us to dwell on the past, or they can propel us forward, allowing us to let go of it, being grateful for all we have in the moment, and looking forward to making a new story we're excited to participate in. Stories change, and so we must change with them. Dreams are like a bedtime story; poems we silently read to ourselves in order to validate and subconsciously make manifest the desires that live in the back of our minds, concealed beneath layers of the truth about our lives.

In dreams, we can say what comes to mind without having to worry about the repercussions, since we are the moderators in the private world of dreams. For instance, if you dream about taking an examination and acing it, the dream may be a reflection of your desire to be at the top of the class and to be chosen as the valedictorian. But when you are wide awake, you are unable to muster the gumption to study for the test in order to fulfill the dream. The dream is telling you what you really want, but perhaps not going so far as to insist that you take steps to ensure you get it. Going even deeper, it is reflecting your unconscious desire for success, while highlighting your apparent subconscious fear of success (or failure) so you can begin to address it on a conscious level.

Dreams are also your mind's way of helping you reach a satisfactory conclusion to a situation that's already transpired. For example, in waking life you may have had a good friend with red hair who abandoned you for some reason, and you've never been able to figure out why. Perhaps, while you'd thought and grieved about it for a while, you were never able to obtain closure or release the emotions arising, so they were suppressed. Eventually, you forgot about it and life went on for you. Then one night, you had a dream you met a person wearing a red handkerchief on their head and you feel threatened. With the feeling of that threat comes an improbable hailstorm. As the dream continues you notice, all of a sudden, you're holding a basket filling up with hail and you toss it at the kerchiefed person's feet. You walk away, and as you do so, you begin floating. You float several miles away where there is no more hail. When you wake up, you feel a sense of relief. Perhaps this feels strange to you, because there's no particular reason for it, given your current lifestyle and social circumstances.

In essence, this dream portrays the grief you felt as a result of the abandonment of your friend (hail), that you'd been holding on to without realizing it (basket). By way of the contemplation you did at the time of the incident, along with the aid of your subconscious over time, you were able to work out the emotion and feel the weight of the grief lifted off of you (floating), which explains the sense of relief upon waking.

Dreams can also help you find solutions to problems that you have been working on for a while, without being able to reach a solution. A favorite story of mine is one told by Albert Einstein about his famous Theory of Relativity. Einstein claimed that he had been touching on the elements of this new theory for some time, but the principles that would mesh it into a coherent theory were still unclear to him. After a while, he had a dream in which he saw several cows lined up close to an electric barbed wire fence, just standing there. He wondered about their being electrocuted, and as he did, he saw a farmer quite a distance away flip a switch to turn on the electricity. Standing close to the fence, Einstein saw all the cows leap backward together at once. Then he walked over to where the farmer was and related to the farmer what he had seen. The farmer told him that he had seen it differently. He said that he'd seen the cows jump back one by one.

Upon waking, Einstein, being the man he was, contemplated the elements of the dream for some time. In these reflections, the principle for the Theory of Relativity came to him. He worked out that the occurrence of an event happening (the cows jumping back, all together vs. one by one) is dependent on the observer (himself vs. the farmer) and the amount of time it takes light to reach the observer's eye (himself close up vs. the farmer at a distance).

So you see from the sum of these examples, that dreams can point to deeper reflections of your subconscious from an event that had happened in the past, or one in the present with respect to future outcomes. Dreams can help you fully express repressed or unexpressed emotions, or to gain a better understanding of a puzzling problems. The time span between the event that affects us in waking life and the dream that provides insight into it can be days, weeks, months or even years, as our minds work through the event or problem. The logical mind says, "Here is the cause, and the effect comes immediately afterward." This can help explain why dreams appear to be so spontaneous and erratic in nature. It's because the language of dreams does not follow the logical mind. It follows the subconscious mind, and the subconscious mind has no concept of linear time. But this still does not answer why we dream. There are five theories that exist to answer that question.

You dream to learn

Have you had dreams in which you've been chased by a dog, or were fighting an enemy or falling off a cliff? This is because your amygdala (uh – MEEG – dah – la), which is the part of the brain that facilitates your fight or flight responses. It's working at its peak during your REM sleep. The amygdala is one of two centers in your brain that regulates your sense of safety in any given moment. The other is the hippocampus. Aside from stress response mediation, it also governs memory storage and emotions. The amygdala catalogues a history of fear responses. But the amygdala has another, surprising function that research has recently uncovered.

Jeffrey Sutton, an assistant professor of psychiatry has stated that the amygdala works overtime, while we sleep. This almond shaped portion of our brains governs many of our waking functions, generating a wealth of electrical activity. This is one of the reasons sleep is so important to us. Without it, our brains literally run out of gas. When we dream, at least one of the functions of the brain activity involved is the support of learning. In dreams, we're also consolidating memories and cataloguing them, in order of importance. By the same process, we may banish certain memories as either undesirable, or not of any particular value.

Research on sleep-deprived rats has demonstrated that they're much less equal to the challenge of running a maze after a sleepless night. Rats who have enjoyed a good night's rest run the mazes in clinical trials with ease, as their brains have had a chance to do the nocturnal work they need to accomplish in order to prepare them for waking life. The same is true of humans, researchers have found. Experiments asking that subjects recall the position of a variety of objects, rapidly projected as they watched, were more readily able to correctly answer questions about their positions after a good night's sleep. As the result of subsequent studies, it was found that those who were subjected to the same clinical trial, when woken up in the midst of REM-sleep, were unable to recall anything about what they'd seen. Those who were awakened in another stage of the sleep cycle were much more likely to recall what had been projected.

Sutton and his associate at the Harvard Medical School, Allan Hobson, discovered that the chemical Acetylcholine was largely responsible for this effect. This powerful chemical promotes both the consolidation and cataloguing of memory in the brain, as we sleep, and provokes our dreams. When the chemical was injected in cats as part of the study, it was found to induce increased dream activity.

The research conducted by Harvard team of Sutton and Hobson may hold the key to mitigating the symptoms of Alzheimer's, which degenerates the memory of people with the disease. By exploring the production of Acetylcholine by brain cells and its early degeneration of Acetylcholine-producing cells in patients with the disease, these researchers are hoping to find a way to predict who will develop the disease and possibly find a way to inhibit its effect on the brains of those who suffer from its degenerative effects.

The modern human brain vs. the primitive human brain

The greatest difference between modern times and the primitive times in which the fight or flight response best served us is that, by and large, we no longer have to fight the elements for food, shelter and escaping death. The system is still working in our brains, however the stimuli which gave rise to its function have decreased. These days the system relates more to a sense of need for emotional survival than physical. If you have trouble understanding your emotions and working through them, then the history of fear responses becomes slightly skewed. You tend to recognize a stressor and react to it, rather than processing the fact that it's actually no immediate threat to you (for example, a work deadline or a person who routinely undermines you at work or in the home). The brain-body's response to this is the stimulation of the adrenal glands that produces a stress hormone called cortisol and presto – you are in fight or flight mode. But since you have no actual immediate threat, despite the primitive machinations of your brain, you must either absorb the stress or find a way to effectively release it. If you don't, the brain does it for you via the amygdala and its role in your dreams.

REM sleep and dreams

It is during REM sleep that your dreams take place. This was proven by Antti Revonsuo, a Finnish cognitive scientist and neuroscience professor at the University of Skovde, Sweden. He also teaches psychology at the Turku University in Finland.   It was his Threat Simulation Theory that led to an understanding of our subconscious mind's role in our dreams. He essentially proved that our dreams serve us as a means of rehearsing our responses to potential threats. In our dreams, we live out scenarios that may present themselves in our waking life and learn, by virtue of these "rehearsals" to defend ourselves in waking life. Stemming from the primitive mind, this function continues to serve us, perhaps giving rise to hypervigilance, but ultimately providing us with necessary learning concerning the identification of possible enemies, or dangerous situations.

During REM sleep, your brain is working in the same way it does when it perceives danger, or a threat. The part of your brain that works to monitor your motor skills also is working at its peak. You may not be moving your limbs, but you are rehearsing for a fight that plays out in the course of a dream. Revonsuo proved that dreams are a theater in which you rehearse your response to a potential threat. You train your reactions – both physical and emotional – during these rehearsals.

You dream to become wise

Your brain limits the number of images which can be stored in your conscious memory. If you remembered every image that your senses have taken in, your brain would be overloaded with information and shut down. Besides this, our brains are actually doing more work for us than we are aware of. Maybe you've seen a spy movie or read a Sherlock Holmes mystery in which the someone's able take in vast amounts of detailed information in a relatively short period of time. It's not just fiction, but based on real people whose job it is to record and retain a large amount of detailed information. They must train to do so, but really they are not learning a new skill. They have trained their conscious memories to work up to what the subconscious mind is already doing without us noticing.

If you are familiar with the idea of subliminal messages, they work in a similar way. The human brain is capable of recording every single bit of detail in our central and peripheral vision, as well as our hearing and our sense of smell. The difference is our being able to remember and place it all. The reason we are not all walking around with the super sensitive sensing skills of Sherlock Holmes is because of: 1. The memory overload that was discussed earlier, 2. A lot of information is not considered important enough to retain for what our brains know to be the necessary items required for survival and most importantly, 3. We have not told our brains otherwise in order to put its super skills to use.

Your brain sorts through memories that have lodged themselves in your subconscious mind and tries to identify which memory it should store and which it should not. It segregates the memories through your dreams. Matt Wilson, a professor at MIT's Center for Learning and Memory, strongly backs this theory. He conducted an experiment on rats where he put them in a maze throughout the day and monitored their neuron patterns. He then observed their neuron patterns during REM sleep. Wilson discovered that the patterns were the same during the rats' REM sleep, as when the rats were running through the maze. He claimed that the brain uses dreams to identify the worthiness of a memory.

Dreaming is Defragmentation

When you buy a new laptop or a desktop, the first thing you do is separate your drives. You create the number of drives you want in the space that is provided by the device. In the same way, your brain also tries to identify the importance of different memories you have stored about your life. Francis Crick and Graeme Mitchison Reverse Learning Theory posits that, in sleep, the brain functions much as a computer does, tossing information that's no longer required for its functioning. Essential, the theory claimed that people dream in order to forget. What they intended is that the brain tries to identify whether the data it contains in the form of memories is useful or not. It tries to identify a connection between the data and to discard memories that don't contribute much to a person's wisdom. Dreaming is a method by which your brain shuffles through your memories in order to identify which connections are important and which are not.

Dreams are your own personal psychotherapist

You may have begun to wonder about the emotional aspects of your dreams. You may raise the question about how dreams serve as your own personal rehearsal to confront surprising and difficult emotions. Ernest Hartmann, a doctor at Tufts (a private research institution), attempted to answer this question. He focused on the learning that happens when a person dreams. He propounded the theory that the difficult emotions people experience while awake are transposed into images when they dream. When you dream, you are dealing with all your difficult emotions in a safe place. This is just like psychotherapy. When you're dreaming, you're on your personal, private therapeutic couch where you can allow your wiser consciousness to deal with emotional imbalance. Through your dreams, you are able to accept certain truths about your emotional state you're unable to while awake.

Sometimes a cigar really is just a cigar

As mentioned above, that pesky cigar is sometimes nothing more than a cigar. Maybe you saw someone smoking it, or maybe you're just craving one. The latest theory (stemming from a 1977 study by Allan Hobson and Robert McCarley of Harvard University), is that dreams have no meaning, whatsoever and that cigars are sometimes nothing more than cigars. Cognitive psychology argues that the brain fires images at random. These images are scenarios that have never been viewed during your waking life. Your dreams are like a film in which the brain has created a scenario that has never been experienced by you consciously, but is the result of the images and experiences being collected and collated into random arrangements that result in what we know as dreams. Theorists believe that your conscious mind tries to attach deep meaning to these images in order to explain them. What's more likely is that these scenarios and images spring from earlier memories stored in the subconscious.

Hobson and McCarley's hypothesis is that of activation and attendant synthesis, in which scientific observation noted distinct differences between the waking and sleeping (specifically during the REM part of the sleep cycle) neuronal activity in the area of the brain stem. Brain activation during REM, with the eyes closed (thus shutting off the brain from external stimuli) was provoked by the shutting down of the thalamus. This part of the brain is a receptor for waking stimuli and ceases to function in the same manner when we sleep. The lower functioning of this part of the brain leads to oscillation, which activates the subconscious to draw on imagery already embedded in the subconscious.

Summation

To sum up, would it not be safe to conclude that all these theories on the purpose and role of dreams may share in common at least some validity? Although on the podium of the ego, there is little wiggle room, it's clear that merit is present in a number of varying scientific explanations for the phenomenon of dreaming. While many people would like to convince themselves and others that there is one only way of explaining dreams, this is seldom the case with any form of empiricism concerning the subconscious mind. There has never been an instance in the history of life on this planet where only one way of viewing things was entirely correct and I don't believe the study of dreams and dreaming is at all different.

Although some theoretical models arguably have greater merit than others, the sum of the whole usually informs a more thoroughgoing understanding, due to the different perspectives in play. You remember Einstein and the cows? It's instructive in terms of what I'm saying here. We now know the world is not flat and that the earth revolves around the sun and not vice versa. and so it's safe to say that the whole truth must be gleaned from not only empiricism, but the full panoply of theoretical approaches to arrive at a representative version of the truth.

There are always a number of ways to go about understanding a mystery in life. There are also a multitude of valid answers that can arise from one mystery. Life is not so cut and dried as to offer one and only one solution for every problem or ambiguity we face. As Einstein demonstrated, the dynamic universe in which we exist is all relative and circumstantial.

Perhaps that's the problem psychologists and analysts face in trying to categorize one purpose for dreaming and why people still know so little about it or can't seem to decide what the exact purpose is. There can be many purposes. It depends upon the context of the dream in relation to the dreamer's personal experience. Over the span of a given time period, one person can have several dreams that each fit into one of the several theories listed previously. They can have one dream in June that relates to playing out a response to a fear or stressor. The next week they may have a dream that is a compilation of all the things their mind has been going over throughout the course of the past few days. In July they may have a dream that plays out an emotion they've been holding on to from an event that occurred the previous year, and was never adequately dealt with. And so on. You are not confined to being one and only one way. Neither has science yet been able to explain phenomena like the experience of Edwin Moses, or even that of Oliver Cromwell, who both experienced premonitions in the context of their prospective dreams which are beyond scientific explanation (so far).

Now that you are aware of the various theories about dreaming, practice making an assertion to yourself as to what a dream's purpose is the next time you have one. Keep a record of your dreams in the form of a dream journal and discover which theory you feel fits each particular dream. It may very well be that your dream serves no purpose and is rather a mishmash of memories and sensory information accumulated from your life experienced. At least it's fun, interesting and perhaps even

57

self-revelatory to analyze your dreams. Let yourself be the judge. The more you practice recording your dreams and analyzing their elements to see if they synch with a deeper part of yourself you'd like to know more about, the more you'll develop a keen sense of what purpose they serve, if any.

Facts about Dreams

You are probably already aware that the dreams you have are fascinating, terrifying, exciting or downright weird. Have you ever been reluctant to share your dreams? Do you feel that you might be alone in dreaming about certain situations or scenarios? Does the nature of your dreams frighten you out of wanting to know what they really mean? Rest assured, you are not the only one, and you have nothing to fear. Theorists have identified these five facts about dreams.

Everyone dreams!
Men, women, babies and even animals dream. People who claim to have a dreamless sleep simply don't remember their dreams after waking up. That doesn't mean they don't dream. Regardless of what they claim or what they do not remember, they dream just as frequently and vividly as the rest of us. Through multiple studies conducted on the nature of dreams over time, it has been proven that every human being has multiple dreams every night, and that each of these lasts for a minimum of 10 minutes to a maximum of forty-five minutes. If measured in years, a human being dreams for close to six years in the span of an average life.

Many of us tend to forget our dreams

Have you ever had a wonderful dream that you had hoped you'd remember in the morning? But when you wake up, you have forgotten the entire dream and still have the nagging feeling that it was wonderful, even expository? Allan Hobson, of Harvard Medical School, as stated that people forget close to 95% of their dreams a few minutes after waking up. When Hobson conducted brain scans of people in the throes of dreaming, it was found that the frontal lobe of the brain, which is essential to storing memory, was inactive. The frontal lobe, so crucial to our waking function, was completely disabled in sleep and able to ignore the nocturnal machinations of other parts of the brain.

You may have pastel colored dreams

It has been found that close to 80% of your dreams are in color. However, there exists a minimal percentage of people who claim to always dream in black and white. There is a slightly higher number of people who have one to several dreams in black and white, and this aspect has been determined to hold some significance.

If you dream in black and white, it suggests that you need to be more objective about how you make your decisions. You may be a little too inflexible in the way you think and therefore, need to find some sort of balance when presented with opposing or contrasting options or opinions. Think about the phrase "He only sees in black and white." Consider the views and opinions of others. You may want to work toward finding a middle ground in your perspectives and beliefs. Another interpretation proposes that black and white dreams are a sign of depression or sadness. You may feel there is not enough to be enthusiastic about in your life.

But research has found that people who are woken up during REM sleep and asked to choose a color from a chart that was synchronous to their dream, they tended to choose pastel colors.

You can control your dreams

Lucid dreaming is a fascinating idea which many believe they actually engage in with regularity. It has been proven that people can control the content and outcomes of their dreams. This is called lucid dreaming. Identified in the early part of the 20th Century by Frederik van Eeden, a Dutch psychiatrist, lucid dreaming is said to be experienced by almost everyone at least once in their lives, but regularly by only 20 % of the population. Research in the 1970s, began to discern the possibility that this type of dreaming could, in fact, occur in the REM stage of the sleep cycle. The clinical community largely dismisses the possibility of lucid dreaming, based on a dearth of empirical support, but research is ongoing.

In the context of a lucid dream, the dreamer is aware that he or she is dreaming, even though asleep. The sensation of dreaming, as opposed to waking life, is discernible and almost palpable to the dreamer. This confers the power to manipulate elements of the dream to some extent and to control the direction it takes. With this ability, it's possible to accomplish some pretty amazing feats! As stated above,

most people experience at least one lucid dream at some
point in their lives, but the percentage of people who
experience them regularly is less than one quarter of the
population. It's possible that most people can experience
the wonder of a lucid dream by training themselves how to
initiate them by way of auto-suggestion. The concept of
Lucid Dreaming is covered in detail in Chapter 4.

Dreams paralyze you

During your REM sleep, the part of your brain that deals
with motor functions is latent. When you have a dream in
which you are flailing your arms about to protect yourself,
you are not doing that in reality. You are immobilized in
your sleep.

Have you ever been chased in a dream? Did you wake up
terrified? Did you find yourself unable to move a muscle?
This is called sleep paralysis. It is not permanent. Sleep
researchers have found that there are two types of sleep
paralysis - one for when you are falling asleep, and one for
when you are waking up. In both cases, your cognizance is
alert and aware in a waking state, but your body is still in a
dormant state of sleep. Essentially, your mind and your
body are out of sync with sleep states and this is why,
although you may feel awake, your body is still inhibited in
its dormant sleep state, where you are not able to move or
speak for as brief a period as a few seconds, or as long as a
few minutes. Upon waking, your body needs a moment to
catch up with your mind.

This immobilization can be pretty terrifying for people
who have not experienced it before or do not know what is

actually happening. This is especially true for those who have just awakened from a nightmare. In fact, since this phenomenon has been part of human life since the human race developed the powers of thought, people long ago believed that when something like this occurred, they were being plagued by nocturnal demons or alien abductors. Henry Fuseli's painting "The Nightmare" depicts those speculative demons and was mostly probably inspired by his own experience of the terror of sleep paralysis. These symptoms, aside from immobilization of speech and movement, can include a chest-crushing feeling and sometimes even hallucinations.

It has been observed that once people are familiar with the real causes of sleep paralysis and what it involves, their fearful experience is greatly reduced (as opposed to say, thinking a demon is sitting on their chest). This phenomenon can occur in about four of every 10 people, so it is a common condition. Some factors possibly linked to the cause of it can include a lack of sleep, a sleep schedule that changes, high volumes of stress, sleeping on your back, substance abuse, and possible medical conditions like bipolar disorder or narcolepsy. If it happens to you frequently, it might be wise to consult a physician a, but remember that on the whole, it is a harmless occurrence that rarely points to underlying disorders.

The way sleep paralysis is, if occurring on a regular basis, is by improving your sleep habits and making sure you get six to eight hours of sleep consistently. Taking steps to relieve stress in your life, especially before bedtime, is also a helpful practice. Remember also that the best sleeping positions for your body are first on your left side, followed by lying on your back. Lying on your stomach or your right side are the least recommended positions. That's because the weight of your lungs puts pressure on the heart, due to their locations in your body. Your stomach's digestive function can also be compromised by lying on your right side.

23 Dream Facts That Won't Send You to Sleep

Since time began, we have been trying to figure out what our dreams mean. Long ago, all dreams were interpreted to be omens, good or bad, about the future, or messages from the gods, even representations of reality. Today, we tend to see dreams in more of a scientific manner but that doesn't stop people from being fascinated by these scenes that take place in their heads over night. Take a look at these 23 facts about dreams:

1. Ancient Romans would submit unusual dreams to those others for interpretation, including members of the Senate.

2. The oldest Dream Dictionary still in existence is the Beatty Papyrus, written about 1350 BC. It was discovered near Thebes.

3. The role of aggression in a dream is influenced by

birth order. Men's dreams will typically be more violent than those of women, but a first-born female's dreams will generally feature more aggressive characteristics. First-born males tend to have dreams that put them in a more positive light than their younger brothers.

4. If you grew up in an era when black and white television was all you had, you will be more likely to dream in the monochromatic scale than a person brought up with a color television.

5. People who are visually impaired dream as well. People who lost their sight later in life, will see visual images, but dreams do not always have to be visual. Blind people who don't have visual dreams will experience them through smell, touch and sound.

6. If you dream of a face, it will be someone you have met or know. You may not know that you have encountered them because, typically, we see hundreds of different faces every day but you will have seen them somewhere, even if only on television, or a movie, or in a photograph.

7. Between 18 and 38% of people claim to have had at least one dream that was a premonition of an event that came to pass, while 70% say they have experienced déjà vu.

Discover the Meaning of Your Dreams and How to Dream
What You Want - Dream Interpretation, Lucid Dreaming, and
Dream Psychology

8. Psychologists say that daydreaming could be related to the dreams you have at night, but that waking and sleeping dreams do not involve the same mental processes.

9. Within about 5 minutes of waking up, most people forget at least 50% of their dream. After 10 minutes, at least 90% is forgotten. However, if you wake up during the REM stage of sleep, you are more likely to remember your dream.

10. Dreams in which you are unprepared, suffering public humiliation, falling, or flying, stem from anxieties you may be experiencing

11. According to the inventor of the sewing machine, Elias Howe, his nightmares contained cannibals that chased him, carrying spears that looked very much like the sewing machine needle he went on to design.

12. Dreams in which you are falling (a common dream theme in mammals) tend to occur in the earlier sleep stages. They are accompanied by muscle spasms which are known as myoclonic jerks.

13. Around 40% of the population suffers from sleep paralysis. This occurs when a person wakes up and recognizes where they are, but can't move for either several seconds, or for as long as one minute.

14. In men's dreams, about 70% of the characters will be men while, in a woman's dreams, the split between male and female will be fairly even.

15. Plato proposed that dreams are actually produced by the function of our internal organs. He referred to the liver as the "biological seat of dreams".

16. Research carried out in a number of studies has found that waking someone at the start of the REM cycle of sleep can lead to hallucinations, irritability and, in some cases, eventual psychosis.

17. William Shakespeare was known for using his dreams to help him move his plot development along and develop the characters in his plays.

18. The Ancient Greeks were convinced that dreams were messages from God and they would, on occasion, sleep in sacred places in an attempt to provoke a significant dream or message.

19. Children's dreams don't tend to be as long as those of adults, but about 40% of their dreams are nightmares. Scientists say this is because dreams are a child's coping mechanism.

20. Studies show that animals dream in the same way humans do.

21. Dream incorporation occurs when sound or stimuli

are included in your dreams. An example would be if your neighbors are playing loud music as you sleep. You may dream of being at a rock concert, actually hearing the music and seeing yourself in the audience (until the racket eventually wakes you up).

22. The word dream is most likely derived from a West Germanic word, "draugmas", which translates to mean phantom, deception or illusion.

23. Children will not dream about themselves and will not see themselves in their dreams until they are about 3 or 4 years of age.

Chapter 2: Dream Interpretation

'The dream is a series of images, which are apparently contradictory and nonsensical, but arise in reality from psychological material which yields a clear meaning.'

- Carl Jung

Probably one of the most widely-known and respected fathers of the field of dream interpretation, Carl Jung was a contemporary and student of Sigmund Freud whose association with him ended over a divergence concerning dream theory. Both a psychologist and psychiatrist, Carl Gustav Jung's contributions to the study of dreams and their role in our lives includes a vast array of writings on the subject. He was also a master of semiotic interpretation and a keen analyzer of symbolic relationships in psychology.

Jung believed that dreams create a bridge between our unconscious and unconscious minds. He claimed that when people dream, there occurs a process in which they're able to adhere to different solutions encountered in waking life. While eschewing the *need* for dream interpretation, his fascination with symbolic meaning leaves us with a vast array of writing on the subject of semiotics and their role in apprehending meaning.

Jung's break with Freud primarily concerned Freud's insistence that dreams were an attempt on the part of the subconscious to conceal trauma, or the true self from the dreamer's conscious awareness. Jung saw dreams as a bridge that was revelatory and hopeful in terms of self-awareness. This decidedly more positive attitude toward the role of dreams was a profound challenge to the Freudian interpretative school, turning it on its head. Jung began to conduct his own research, adding an important spiritual component in which Freud had shown little interest.

It was Jung's contention that dreams could be properly interpreted only by the dreamer. He further suggested that there were certain common symbols that could be interpreted and applied generally, but that there were other symbols unique to the dreamer that could be interpreted in a highly personal manner. Regardless, it was Carl Jung's belief that whether dreams were interpreted or analyzed, or not, that they served a unique function in the human mind, transporting hidden meaning and understanding to the waking consciousness of the dreamer, acting as a conduit of the subconscious.

Human beings long for wholeness. The wounds of life can lay dormant inside us, as suppressed memories and concealed triggers that can make that longing an elusive quest few of us are able to attain to. But Jung believed the possibility of human intellectual and spiritual integrity lay in exploiting dreams as the binding agent between the subconscious and conscious minds. He believed that dreams had the power to heal human dis-ease by uniting these seemingly separate realities, which in truth, form part of a whole.

A precursor to Joseph Campbell and arguably the most intense influence on his work, Jung spent a great deal of time exploring the world of religion and spirituality in relation to psychology. He was set on this path as a boy, when after taking his first communion, he said he felt "nothing". He wondered how this might be in the midst of the profundity of the Mass, with its imagery of the salvific work of the incarnation of God in Christ. How was it, he wondered, that he could take in his mouth a host of bread (representing the Body of Christ) and not be spiritually transported? This led him to wonder how the Mass and the world of religion in general might be transformed by psychological analysis, employing the power of semiotics to intensify its inherent strength.

The Mass and other liturgical forms in world religions are filled with symbols and signs and it was these Jung explored to interpret their symbolic riches as psychological realities that might help people move toward the wholeness we all seek. Unfortunately, this aspect of his work has been the subject of a great deal of hostility from a variety of religious commentators, casting him as an enemy of the Church and a pretender to the throne of God. In fact, all Jung wanted to was find a way to cause the Mass and its Communion to resonate for those who, like himself as a young boy, had not felt the intended magic of the Body of Christ. He sought to transform religious symbolism into a semiotic world that those other than theologians might gain access to and thus, the healing promised by the soteriology (salvation theology) of the Church.

Jung's exploration of symbols as doors to meaning otherwise unavailable to us, is the pioneering basis for our understanding of their power in modern dream interpretation. His work illuminates the undefinable by creating touch points of definition which continue to influence the study of dreams and also, the project of pursuing human wholeness through the integration of the conscious and subconscious minds.

There are numerous dream dictionaries on the market that can be used to interpret the meaning of various objects, animals and scenarios present in dreams. Many of these symbols find their universal interpretations in the ancient world, or primitive cultures. Many of them, though, have been expanded in their interpretation by the work of people like Sigmund Freud, Carl Jung and Joseph Campbell. This chapter seeks to help you find out how you can interpret your dreams and understand what they mean.

Do your dreams have a hidden meaning?

It has been said that the most meaningful dreams occur between 2:00 a.m. and 7:00 a.m. This makes sense in light of the way in which human brain processes information in the sleep cycle. This will be discussed in more depth in Chapter 3. However, all this is based on the assumption of a regular sleep schedule that gets you to sleep by between 9:00 p.m. and 11 p.m. The amount of time you sleep and the regularity of your sleep schedule can both impact the quality of your dreams and their quantity, also.

Have you ever had a dream in which you were rolling off a cliff? You might have been rolled off the bed by someone at the very same time, or rolled off it, yourself. Your subconscious mind is conveying a message to you in the form of a dream and asking you to realize that you are rolling off your bed. It is also possible that you are going through stage I of sleep in which this feeling of falling commonly occurs, so much so, in fact, that it has earned a medical name known as *hypnic myoclonia*, translated from Greek meaning "sleep" and "muscle twitch." Typified by the hypnic jerk, or sleep start, this phenomenon can be accompanied by accelerated heart rate and breathing and is described by those who've experienced it as not unlike falling over the lip of a chasm.

Dreams related to the physical environment you are in have little or no significance as far as their meaning is concerned. For instance, if you were to have a dream in which a loud noise was made, it will not have any drastic impact on your life. Your subconscious mind sometimes incorporates your ·physical environment and the happenings in that environment into your dreams. For instance, you may dream you are on a game show and are trying to buzz in to answer. In reality, the baby monitor might have been buzzing. It could be that your subconscious is sending you a message asking you to wake up because of the noise, or simply that you are reaching a point in your sleep cycle where you are closest to being awake and the noise is permeating to the lighter level of that subconscious state you are in.

It may also be the case that while that particular dream you are having may have some significance, the stimulus that you are getting from your physical environment is intruding into your sleep and being processed as a dream. The external stimulus of the baby monitor, while your body sleeps, is recognized by your brain as a dream, when what's really occurring is dream incorporation, as discussed earlier.

There are certain elements often found in the dreams of many people. These dreams elicit a wide range of emotions. These dreams can be interpreted easily.

Common dreams and their interpretations

The following are some examples of the most common dream themes, experienced by people all over the world. People may experience these themes in the course of dreaming only once, or perhaps, several times. These dreams may also manifest as a recurring theme, which expands and changes over time, while the central plot of the dream remains static and familiar. We'll talk about recurring dreams in more depth a little later on.

Falling Dreams

Falling dreams are very common and most people will experience them at some point in their lives. Dreams on this theme also tend to be very memorable and those who dreaming of falling will often recount the details of them to others.

These dreams indicate you're afraid of losing or letting go of something. They also indicate that you're anxious about failing, following a successful event in your life. Ultimately, falling dreams suggest a loss of control. Whether it's falling from a cliff, a building, a rooftop, an airplane, or some higher ground (which are all elements subject to further interpretation), in the dream, you typically have no control and nothing to hang onto.

Falling dreams can mean you're feeling overwhelmed, whether at school, work, or in your home environment, as well as in the context of personal relationships. The following is a short list of possible life realities that falling dreams can be sub-conscious reactions to.

Cathleen O'Connor, PhD, says that dreams about falling may have nothing to do with your subconscious mind at all; that they may, in fact, be based entirely on physiological realities which assert themselves as we sleep. Our hearts slowing down, coupled with slowed breathing are signs that we are "falling" asleep. As this occurs, our bodies may protest with a hypnic jerk. In short, a falling dream (occurring on the cusp of sleep), may be nothing more than a subconscious response to a physical reality.

Insecurity

A sense of precarity, instability, and/or a lack of confidence can all be indicated by dreams about falling.

You may fear that you are losing your job or your home. Also possibly indicated are feelings of shame, inferiority, vulnerability and low self-esteem. You could be afraid of not being able to live up to other people's expectations or the standard prescribed for a given circumstance. If you have had certain demands put on you recently, it would not be surprising for you to experience a falling dream.

Reckless behavior

Recently engaging in reckless behavior can also provoke your subconscious to produce a dream that you're falling. Making poor behavioral decisions, binge drinking, or a general sense that you lose control of yourself too regularly can cause your subconscious to issue this common wake up call. You probably don't care to deal with "acting out" behavior in your waking life, but your subconscious is well aware of that and may be handing you a penalty card.

Falling dreams, like all dreams, have in them kernels of universal symbolism, but must also be interpreted in light of the dreamer's context. A falling dream experienced by someone of considerable economic means may point to concerns about the stability of financial holdings. A farmer's dream about falling may have more to do with worries about the quality of the harvest, due to the unstable weather patterns. A teenager's dream may have to do with success at school, while an athlete's may point to a fear of losing an upcoming race, or regret about just having lost one. In the field of dream interpretation, context and personalization must always accompany the examination of the scenario or symbol's universally recognized significance.

Nude Dreams

Dreams about being naked in a public setting is another universal theme, experienced by most people. Dreams of finding yourself suddenly nude in the midst of an important business meeting, walking down the street, in the corridors of your old high school, or at church are exceptionally common.

Vulnerability and Fear of Exposure

Feeling vulnerable, or as though others will find out something about you or your life you don't want them to know can provoke dreams of unexpected, sudden, or socially inappropriate nudity. Nude dreams can also be a sign that you're afraid of intimacy, or entering into a relationship in which intimacy may be called for. Feeling helpless or judged by others is another circumstances that can provoke nude dreams. Fear of rejection by others is a further psychological pretext for nude dreams.

Clothing, while necessary for warmth and protection from the elements, is also a way for us to disguise and cover ourselves in other ways. Clothing can be used as a means of camouflage, or costume. In this respect, it's useful as a means of concealing our identities from those we don't know. We choose our manner of dressing our bodies and the messages we send with our clothing resonates with others. While the business suit sends a message of masculine economic power, it also serves to send a message of the same gender's sexual potency, in employing the necktie. This important component of business attire is (whether wittingly or not), a symbol of the male penis. The form-fitting dress may be perceived as sexual come on, but it also sends a strong message of sexual independence and confidence. These are only two examples of how the way we dress our bodies can resonate with others as subconscious, or even explicit messages about who we are and how we wish to be perceived.

When, in our dreams, we're stripped of our clothing, the metaphor speaks to a fear of exposure. Physical nakedness is redolent of the vulnerability of the human animal. Without our protective layer of clothing, we become exposed to the elements, to the eyes of others and thus, to their ridicule and judgement – even attack.

Arrogance and the humility of nudity

Dreams have a way of revealing to us things about ourselves we subconsciously understand are in need of change, or reform. What we're unwilling to acknowledge in our waking lives, our subconscious points to as we dream. Dreams provide us with subconscious insight that doesn't filter up to our conscious minds. We have ways and means of distracting ourselves from the hard work of change, but if that still, small voice is alive, it's at its loudest in our dreams.

Naked dreams may be telling us that we need to examine our attitudes toward others. The fear of exposure made manifest in the realm of dreams can indicate that we're aware of our shortcomings, but perhaps unable to name them. Sometimes, we harbor the unfortunate belief that we're superior to others and nakedness in dreams can serve as an illustration of our fear of this coming to light. We know we're wrong. We just can't admit to ourselves that we have this belief (even though others may point it out to us, to our dismay). Our waking denial is worked out in our dreams and is the foundation of personal reflection and hopefully, self-improvement in this respect.

Freedom of Expression

Nudity in dreams can also mean that you're a free spirit, unapologetic in your actions and beliefs. Your self-confidence and self-acceptance make it possible for you to feel just as comfortable naked as clothed. With nothing to hide and no sense of superiority in confrontation of others, you are at peace with yourself and the world around you. Honest, open and carefree, you're free as a bird, unfettered by the psychological detritus far too many people carry around as a burden.

You model the "naked truth" and have no need of deceptive costumes or disguises. Perhaps, alternatively, you're reaching an understanding that others aren't as fortunate as you are, in this regard, and your dream's nudity expresses your desire that they come to be as you are – free.

Attention-seeking

Feeling as though we're being ignored can lead us to a variety of unfortunate life circumstances. One of these is indulging in attention-seeking behaviors that others may find annoying, or distracting. Clothing can be a means of seeking attention, if we dress in outlandish ways in order to be more fully visible. Being loud, dominating conversations and indulging in outrageous public behaviors are other ways people can seek attention.

Being nude in dreams can either express your desire to be noticed by others (or someone in particular), or point to the fact that you're aware of indulging in overt attention-seeking behaviors that may be damaging your relationships with others, or your general reputation. In this instance, it's an important red flag you should pay attention to.

Floating/Flying Dreams

Another universally common dream involves flying or floating. The dream can feature either action and include a sense of weightlessness, release and freedom. You may be floating over the earth and viewing the activities taking place there, or you may be floating over yourself, as you sleep. You may also be fleeing a threat.

Some flying dreams involve the resolution of a threat, or undesirable circumstance in which you seek resolution by literally flying away. Flying and floating dreams tend to be interpreted in exactly the opposite way falling dreams are, depending on the circumstances the dreamer's currently in, or has recently been in.

Flying quickly and high above the ground, with an overwhelming sense of control and exhilaration can indicate that you're feeling confident and optimistic. Alternatively, flying closer to the ground and experiencing difficulty in gaining altitude can indicate you feel held back; unable to achieve daylight between you and whatever's holding you back. But a steady pace, at a low altitude can also mean that you're content with the way things are.

Flying backwards may indicate that you're in a nostalgic mood, hoping to connect with the past and perhaps learn from it, concerning the present and future. Being afraid of flying, as the dream unfolds, means you may fear the heady exhilaration of success and further, that what's before you is a little scary. That doesn't mean you shouldn't do it. It means you'd rather not acknowledge the emotion in your waking life and are working it out in your subconscious. A flying dream may represent a green light and a message that you shouldn't fear change.

Control

By flying with ease and enjoying the landscape you are cruising over, this version of the flying dream is your subconscious mind's way of telling you're in charge and well in control of the situation. Having risen above obstacles and challenges presented to you, you're enjoying the success you've earned. If you are able to control your flight's direction, altitude and speed, it means you're experiencing a sense of personal power and growth.

New Perspective

Looking down at the world from an airplane presents a very different perspective. Moving at high speeds through the air, at an altitude of thousands of feet is a peak experience for this reason. Flying dreams can also represent an expanding worldview, or widened perspective, which is working to make your world a more vibrant place. Flying dreams can also reveal that you should be looking at the big picture and not sweating the small stuff, or details. Viewing the landscape from above allows an increased and varied perspective that can reveal the whole truth about various situations and realities in your life.

Freedom

Many people wish they possessed the power of flight. They look at birds with envy, desiring the ability of these creatures to soar through the air. I suppose that's what led humans to invent aviation and even space exploration. The truth is, human beings have always been fascinated by flight. As earth bound creatures, life can challenge us with the sensation of being stuck to the earth. Flying dreams gift us with the message that all things are possible and that our circumstances (especially when they involve sudden lift off) can change in an instant, freeing us from what troubles us in life. As most of us know, awakening from a flying dream can bring with it the sensation that we're just getting started and that life is yet full of opportunities. This uplifting message sent by flying in our dreams is one we can build on to live our lives more fully and successfully.

Dreams of Death

"I was in a forest - dense, gloomy fantastic, gigantic boulders lay about among huge jungle-like trees."

- Carl Jung

This is Jung's preamble to prophetic dream he experienced, presaging the death of his mother. In the dream, the foreboding forest he finds himself in the midst of is quiet, until suddenly, an enormous wolf crashes through the underbrush, confronting him with its vast jaws, open to carry away its prey.

In his analysis of the dream, Jung recognizes the universal symbol of the Huntsman. This shadowy, semiotic figure is another version of the grim reaper in dream symbolism, sent to bear away a soul in the jaws of its acolyte, the wolf.

The morning following Jung's dream, he received the sad news that his mother had passed away.

While not all dreams about death are created equal, Jung's ability to discern the symbolism of his own dream, led him, in retrospect, to recognize the dream and its contents as a premonition. While his dream is highly symbolic, other dreams about death may not be quite so esoteric and refer more directly to our own, personal attitudes toward and fear of death.

Dreaming of your own death is another dream theme common to people everywhere. A dream of dying can scare the living hell out of us and there's even an old belief that if we don't wake up before the moment we die, in our dreams, we will actually die. It's comforting that this is not the case, as we all know. All the same, the death dream theme can leave us with an uncomfortable sensation for days after experiencing it, in sleep.

It's helpful to remember that dreams, while often symbolic, can sometimes mean nothing. However, in the case of the death theme, it's clear your subconscious is trying to reach your waking mind, in order to send a rather strong message. The profundity of death as part of our lives is a source of anxiety for many (if not most) people. Embracing death as part of our lives, though, can lead us to make peace with it as a natural stage in the cycle of human life. Everything dies and so shall we all.

Western society tends to shove death into a dark corner, where it's rarely discussed. When its shadow passes over our lives, we dispense with it as rapidly as possible, shoving loved ones in heavy wooden boxes, or burning them to be placed in fancy pottery urns, as quickly as we can. We like to get death over with, because thinking about it reminds us of our own mortality. It's enlightening to consider the approach to death in other cultures.

But even in North America, the people of New Orleans have a unique attitude toward death, inviting it into their daily lives, due to the precarious nature of life in that city, since the time it was established. Yellow fever, floods, hurricanes and other human tragedies have beset New Orleans for centuries and so death is like a visiting cousin – always expected and always welcomed. Even their funerals include dancing, as the corpse is laid to rest and the funeral party (or second line) leaves the graveyard to celebrate life.

New Orleans is also home to the Skull and Bones gangs. Dressed in black costumes painted with white skeletons, these gangs go door to door in the wee hours of Mardi Gras morning, banging on people's doors to awaken them so they don't miss one minute of the most important day of the year. As they wake everyone up, they call out, "You next!", meaning "you will be the next to die". The implication is that life is short, so "get up and join the fun" reminds people that there are only so many Mardi Gras mornings in the span of a human life and that they're to be relished. Death comes for us all and in New Orleans, that knowledge is part of what makes the city's slogan "laissez les bontemps roulez" (let the good times roll) so poignant. Who knows when *this* good time will be our last?

New Beginnings

Just as the spring follows winter, new life follows death. Life is an eternal cycle, in all its manifestations. For this reason, dreaming of your own death can be interpreted positively. This dream theme can symbolize inner change, transformation, self-discovery and positive transitions in your psyche and your life in general. It's possible that you are going through a phase of becoming more spiritually enlightened. So dreaming of your death is a way of subconsciously working out that you're moving on from an old way of being, or an old way of life and leaving the past behind you. Destructive behavior, bad habits, a change of location or lifestyle, are all circumstances that might provide a pretext for this dream theme to occur.

Wake-up Call

Dreaming about your own death can also serve as a means for your subconscious to get your conscious mind's attention. You may be either vaguely or acutely aware of life realities that require your urgent attention, but for one reason or another, aren't addressing them. Procrastination and avoidance can be roadblocks to improving situations holding you back. Important to consider is the mood of the dream. Were you mourning yourself? Were you suddenly dead, accompanied by the sensation that you were watching yourself die? These can be signs that you need to pay attention to something in your life that needs change. That could be anything from addiction, to a job you hate, to a toxic or undermining relationship.

Coping with Death

It's also entirely possibly that your subconscious is finding a way for you to more effectively deal with the idea of your eventual demise. As said above, Western society has a shaky relationship with the Grim Reaper and your dream of death may help you move closer to a healthy relationship with this inevitable visitor.

Fear of death can compel us to eschew risk-taking that can enhance our experience of living, by making us overly careful. Some of us may be willing to step out of our everyday lives to take a vacation, because we're afraid of flying. We may be afraid to go out at night, due to a fear of strangers. Anxiety about death, regardless of where we are in our journeys can be a life-killer that makes our worlds small, strained and unfulfilling. By dreaming of our own death, we may be subconsciously working out these fears and finding a way to resolve them and our crippling anxieties around the mystery of life ending.

Death of a loved one

In dreaming of a loved one's death, you may be subconsciously admitting you lack a quality in this person which you desire, but can't articulate. This version of the death dream can also mean that you genuinely fear your loved one will die, or that you love this person so much, you can't imagine life without them. As with the dream about personal death, this dream is rooted in fear and anxiety and calls on the dreamer to develop a healthier relationship with death as an integral part of life.

As we've witnessed in Carl Jung's dream of his mother's death, though, dreaming about the death of a loved one may presage an unwelcome event.

Chasing Dreams

Another universal dream theme is that of being chased by a shadowy, unknown figure. The figure chasing you may also be someone you know, but the face is usually obscured. You can identify them only by other physical characteristics, like size, gender, or a favorite article of clothing. Dreams about being chased, or chasing are in fact the most commonly experienced dreams, shared by people around the world, in every imaginable cultural setting.

The general interpretation of chasing dreams is your sense of threat. Chasing dreams can also mean you're avoiding a situation, important task, event, or person. Again, anxiety and fear are the root causes of this type of dream.
.

The best way to interpret your chasing dream is taking note of as many other factors of the dream as possible. Who or what is it that is chasing you? Look up the meaning of the figure chasing you in your dream dictionary. If you recognize the pursuing figure, consider the nature of your relationship with that person and what the relationship means in the big picture of your life. These factors will help you interpret why you've had the dream, particularly if it recurs frequently, with similar features.

When practicing lucid dreaming, you will be able to understand this is a dream. By using lucid dreaming techniques, you'll eventually be able to control events in the dream, so you can turn around and confront whatever it is that's chasing you and ask it why you're being chased. Consider also the distance between you and your pursuer. This will tell about your proximity to the issue being worked out in the dream. The problem will not go away if the pursuer is gaining on you. If you are widening the gap, though, then it speaks to your ability to successfully distance yourself from the problem, or that the problem is fading away.

Avoidance

The chasing dream may also be your subconscious chiding you for avoiding a situation you need to confront. If you're experiencing fight or flight in the course of the dream, this may further indicate that you have current challenges coping with fear, stress, and other exciting or stimulating situations. Your chasing dream may be pointing out that you have a tendency to run away and avoid issues you're uncomfortable addressing.

If you're doing the chasing

In this role reversal of the typical synopsis, the dream may be focusing on your ambitious nature and your drive to pursue your goals (or someone you're romantically interested in). This version of the chasing dream could be telling you to go after your goals (or your romantic interest). Alternatively, it could mean you may be falling behind in some areas of your life, due to the fact you have the waking sensation of needing to catch up. Being the pursuer in the chasing dream can thus be your subconscious telling you to get down to it.

Dreams about school, exams and time being of the essence

Taking a test or examination in a dream can imply you feel unprepared from some aspect of your waking life that you have just started working on or are about tackle. You do not feel up to the challenge, or you feel you're lacking some essential qualities necessary to meet the challenge. This could be due to a tendency to procrastinate in your waking life. You could be holding on to feelings of guilt for failing to prepare for an important event, missing an appointment, or not meeting your goals, due to your own actions.

A sensation that you lack sufficient time to arrive at a destination, or complete a task, or that you're unprepared for an examination can also point to anxiety on your part about some aspect of your life.

Lack of confidence

Being a worry wart can really hold you back in life. If you have a tendency to fearfully, for no good reason, project worst case scenarios and always expect the worst, a dream about school, lack of time, or taking an examination can mean you need to build up your confidence to a level that's more supportive of your success.

If you're someone who "hopes for the best, but expects the worst," you may entertain the self-destructive habit of steeling yourself for what you believe are inevitable blows. Perhaps this is because if you believe that if you "expect nothing, you'll not be disappointed". The crucial point you're missing in doing this, is that you may be setting yourself up for failure before you even get started. You're selling yourself short by worrying too much about not meeting other people's or your own expectations. You may be even considered a "people pleaser" due to your fear of letting others down. By failing an examination in a dream, arriving late for an appointment, or even finding yourself wandering the halls of your high school naked, unprepared, or late for class, you may be expressing your desire to hold yourself back, due to a subconscious fear of failure, or disappointment. This may indicate you feel unprepared to move to the next level of your relationship, or career.

Fear of Failure

This type of dream may also indicate that you're overly anxious about a real life test, business meeting, date, or interview. This anxiety can merge into your dream life in the form of taking a test. Often, however, people who have such dreams will not be likely to fail a test in real life. It can simply be an expression of the person's over-preparedness or excess anxiety.

Common dreams are a fascinating subject for researchers. Research has found that human beings from a vast array of different cultures have experienced a variety of these dreams. Some psychologists advance the theory that human beings have these common dreams due to the mundane interactions that they have with others on a regular basis, common in all societies. These can be everything from brushing their teeth to visiting the grocery store, to sex. Others say the reason these dreams are so common is because they often relate to a sense of anxiety, which, along with an array of other emotions, is common throughout the world.

Suzanne Bergmann has been a professional dream worker for almost two decades and is also a licensed psychologist. She says that many of our most common, universal dream themes reflect the collective unconscious posited originally by Jung. Underlying our individuality as human beings is a vast pool of shared human experience which gives rise to globally shared fears and anxieties, arising from the common aspects of our lives. Our emotions, in dreams, come to life as imagery and scenarios that give them shape, investing them with our subconscious desire to derive meaning from life itself.

In 1998, a conference of dream workers was held in Oahu, Hawaii, under the banner of the Association for the Study of Dreams. In her keynote address to the conference, Dr. Patricia Garfield offered participants outlines of six dreams, drawn from a variety of historical periods. Her audience was asked to guess from where these dreams hailed and in what century they were dreamed. Dr. Garfield discovered that, even though the conference was for an association of dream analysis professionals, few were able to identify the country or origin, or historic setting of the six dreams offered. This example readily illustrates the universality and timelessness of human dreams.

The way to arrive at the fullest and most worthwhile interpretation of these universal dreams is to consider the mood and explore where it may also apply to your waking life, when you feel the emotions you experienced in the dream most often. It could be a literal expression of your reality or it could be metaphorical. Take into account all the variables extant in your dream scenario. Research the colors, distances, orientation, landscapes, shapes of people or things, and any repetitive actions that occur to gain further insight and specificity. Consider the context of your life and cultural setting, remembering always that dreams, while they may be universal, are also individual. This is key to accurate and helpful interpretation.

Recurring Dreams

Recurring dreams are those which play out in the same way and in the same locations, with the same elements, a number of times. Almost as though following a script, a recurring dream becomes recognizable and even comforting to the dreamer. While they sometimes become more elaborate over time, the course of the dream's action will generally follow the same trajectory, each and every time you have it. Essentially they are dreams that are almost identical in content and, featuring little variation, occurring repeatedly over a span of time that could be a week, months, or even years. These types of dreams are pretty common, often caused by a particular life situation, transitional phase in life, or a problem that keeps coming back again and again. Recurring dreams may also refer to the distant past and an unresolved problem, even from childhood.

Remember that dreams can act as guides to teach you something about yourself. Most often we wake up from dreaming and go about daily life, giving little thought to the dreams we've had. That is, if we can even remember anything we've dreamed at all. The reason a dream occurs repeatedly is that it contains the very powerful message that it will not go away until you are able to do something about it. The repetitious nature of the dream insists that you pay attention and confront the issue it's trying to resolve in the subconscious. Often, recurring dreams can be nightmarish or frightening in context and content, which is another way to get you to notice them.

Dreams like these can shine a light on personal weaknesses, fears, or a personal inability of ability to cope with something particular in your life, whether it's in the past or the present. This could be some of the most important information about yourself you'll ever learn. Recurring dreams may point to a conflict, circumstance or event that remains unresolved. However, once this is addressed and has received the necessary reflection and subsequent closure, they will stop occurring. Dreams you have repeatedly may also be calling on you to seek out the help of a psychotherapist in order to get to the bottom of what your subconscious is attempting to draw your attention to. This is particularly counselled if the dream is disturbing, features violence, or other circumstances that trouble you unduly.

While 60 to 70% of adults experience recurring dreams at some time in their lives, more women than men have them. Recurrent dreams often feature some of the most universal themes (as outlined above), but they're generally associated with a lower level of psychological wellbeing. Antonio Zadra, associate professor of psychology at the University of Montreal, conducted a study in 1996 which revealed that many recurring dreams feature negative content and indicate stressors and repressed memories. If this is the case, the need for clinical intervention may be indicated, as negative recurring dreams represent your subconscious mind's attempt to tell your something important.

But negative dreams may serve the purpose of subconsciously pressing the dreamer toward enhanced achievement. Especially in the case of a dream which features failing an examination, the dream may indicate that the student's concern about succeeding eventually translates into a higher test score. Essentially, the negative content of the dream is an expression of the student's strong desire to succeed. When such a desire is in play, the student is (generally speaking) an exemplary one, focused on academic success and achieving the best possible result.

Zadra's research has also revealed that recurring dreams can serve the purpose of subconscious resolution of past traumas. With each recurrence of the dream "script", the dreamer moves closer to eventual resolution, as the conscious mind begins to actively examine the dream's contents and understand what the script is addressing. There is a therapeutic component to some recurring dreams, by which the dreamer comes to a place of healing through the work of the subconscious on addressing the trauma and resolving its effects on the dreamer.

In the case of PTSD (Post Traumatic Stress Disorder) the recurrence of a dream which features a central image or theme can indicate the need for therapeutic help. While many people who suffer serious trauma are unwilling to address the severity of the experience, the psychological repercussions can last for years, decades, or perhaps even persist through a lifetime. Whether the source of the trauma was an assault, a series of assaults (as in the case of domestic abuse) or an experience of war, PTSD sufferers often don't seek treatment, due to the stigma attached to therapy and mental illness. Often, people with PTSD won't even recognize that they're suffering, or will minimize the impact of the trauma on their psychological health, to the detriment of themselves and those around them.

Jung viewed the experience of recurring dreams instigated by a traumatic experience as completely different from any other kind of dream. He also recognized that dreams like these were processed differently in those who'd suffered serious trauma and represented a psychological shift. In writing of recurring dreams triggered by trauma in his book, *Children's Dreams*, he pointed out that dreams are rarely the re-living of a life experience, except in the case of egregious shock to the psychic system. In this case, dreams are precisely the re-living of the traumatic experience, in vivid detail, adding to the sufferer's stress and anxiety in confrontation of the real life experience.

Therapeutic assistance in integration and "metabolizing" the content the of the traumatic experience by working with those suffering from recurring dreams about it, was already being practiced by Jung 75 years ago. This makes him a pioneer in the treatment of PTSD, at the time yet unnamed. He recognized that there was a strong physical component to experiences involving shock, implicating the nervous system, and that this played a major part in the enduring symptomology of the condition. His work with an English Army officer, though, revealed that by transforming the trauma into symbols that represented its manifest content, PTSD patients were more readily able to absorb their experiences. This made them able to finally resolve the trauma and move on in their lives, as healthy, whole people.

Jung's work is the basis for the new field of Somatic (bodily) Experiencing, which is being developed to help those who have suffered from trauma, and to overcome both the physical and psychic residue of their experiences.

The method takes a holistic approach to trauma, by integrating the shock to the nervous system and biological function into the treatment of the psychological impacts attending.

Some Common Dream Symbols and their Meanings

Our dreams are written in a language that is only readable by the unconscious mind. This is a language inaccessible to us while we're awake. Luckily, dreams contain symbols subject to interpretation, enabling us to understand what they mean. There isn't any rulebook that contains definitions and many of these meanings derive from a variety of cultural understandings about archetypes and their meanings. The following interpretations can help you to begin to understand the personal meanings of your own dreams:

1. **Animals** - sometimes represent the part of your psyche that is the most connected to survival and nature. If you are being chased or hunted down by a predatory animal, it suggests that you may be repressing emotions, such as aggression or fear.

2. **Babies** - these can quite literally mean that you want a child of your own; they can also signify that you are lonely, vulnerable, or have a need

to feel loved. They can also signify a new beginning.

3. **Clothes** – dreams of clothes provide a way for you to see yourself as you want others to, or indicate how you feel others may perceive you. Dreams of shabby clothing could signify you feel worn out or unattractive, while a dream in which you change what you're wearing could signify a change in your lifestyle.

4. **Crosses** – the meaning of dreams with crosses in them depends on your religious beliefs. Some interpretations include symbolic balance, death or the end of a phase in your life. The circumstances of the whole dream can help to truly interpret and define the meaning.

5. **Faulty machinery** - a dream of faulty machinery is a symbol of the language center being closed while you sleep, which makes it difficult for you to do anything. These can also be representative of anxiety about your performance.

6. **Food** - this is a symbol of knowledge. Food feeds the body, while knowledge feeds the brain. On the other hand, you could be really, really hungry or are on a very strict diet.

7. **Demons** - these are evil entities that tend to signify an emotion that you are repressing. It may be that you have a secret desire to change for the better.

8. **Hair** - Dreams of hair signify sexuality. If the dream is of abundant hair, it signifies virility,

while a dream in which the hair is being cut off means a loss of libido. Hair loss dreams can also be a fear of losing your hair.

9. **Hands** - nine times out of ten, there will always be hands in a dream. If the hands are tied, it could represent a feeling of futility while washing hands is a symbol of guilt.

10. **Houses** - there are several interpretations possible, but if you see a whole building, it is representative of the inner psyche. Seeing each individual floor or room of the building can be symbolic of different memories, emotions and meaningful events

11. **Killing** - this doesn't mean that you hold a secret desire to kill; instead, it is representative of a deep desire to change a part of your personality. It can also signify deep hostility towards another person.

12. **Marriage** – this could be a desire to get married or it could be a merger between the masculine and feminine sides of your psyche.

13. **Missing your flight** – or any other form of transportation, signifies frustration over a missed opportunity. This is a common dream in people who are struggling to make a big decision about something.

14. **Money** – dreams about money can be a symbol of self-worth. If you are exchanging money it signifies that you are going through changes in life.

15. **Mountains** – these are obstacles. If your dreams involve you successfully getting to the top of the mountain, it signifies achievement, while if your dream sees you standing and viewing the landscape from the top of the mountain, it can signify that you are reviewing your life without any prejudice.

16. **People** - dreaming of other people is a reflection of your psyche and could be representative of parts of your personality.

17. **Televisions and radios** – these symbolize communication between your unconscious and conscious minds.

18. **Roads** - dreaming of roads is a symbol of your life's direction and might be a hint that you need to start questioning the path you are currently taking.

19. **Schools** – these are common in young children and teens but when an adult dreams of a school it could be signifying that you are looking to understand yourself based on the lessons you have learned in life. (See also schools, exams and time being of the essence).

20. **Teachers** – these signify authority figures who have the power to help you.

21. **Teeth** - these are commonly seen in dreams. If you are dreaming of losing your teeth, it could be that you fear becoming older and unattractive in the eyes of other people. The root of dreams about teeth might also be literal dental problems.

22. **Being physically trapped -** this is a common theme in nightmares and is a reflection of your inability to either make a choice, or escape from a specific situation in real life.

23. **Vehicles -** These signify the level of control you feel you have over your own life. Try to remember if you were driving the vehicle, if it was out of control, or someone else was driving. These different versions indicate a fuller understanding of the dream's meaning.

24. **Water -** dreams of water are symbols of your unconscious mind. If the water is a calm pool, it is a reflection of inner peace, while rough seas may suggest you're uneasy about something.

When Does a Dream Symbol Have Meaning?

Not all the elements of your dreams have an unconscious meaning. Some of them serve as a backdrop to those elements which *are* significant, just as they might serve the same purpose on the stage of a theater. In order to accurately identify which symbols are important, it's important that you keep a dream diary. Write your dreams in the present tense, as if you were living the dream at the time of writing, underlining anything you feel is central to the theme and has particular meaning. Refer to the symbols I have listed above and see if you can work out what your dream may be trying to tell you. Don't forget that all symbols must be taken in context of the whole dream and with those things that may be going on in your life at the moment.

Purchasing a quality dream dictionary is also a very good idea. I've covered some universal themes and symbols in this book, but finding a dream dictionary which has some basis in the work of Freud, Jung, or both is a good idea. It's also a good practice to explore the dream symbolism of other cultures, particularly aboriginal ones. It's in these cultures, in which is preserved primordial knowledge which predates the written record, that the most ancient understanding of symbols may be found. While these may require some adaptation to modern understandings, the raw semiotic form is usually the one closest to the subconscious truth about the symbol's appearance in your dreams.

Apprehending a working understanding of how symbols speak to us in dreams is a not only fascinating, but a solid foundation for learning to interpret and analyze our dreams. This brings us to the next station of our exploration of dreams and understanding them.

How to Analyze Your Dreams

The biggest myth about the analysis of dreams is that there are firm rules that need to be followed in order to interpret them. This is not necessarily the case. As stated earlier, while some symbols in dreams have universally accepted meanings, others may be unique to the dreamer. Nearly every element in a dream comes with not one, but several alternative meanings, so that an interpreter (soon to be you) can derive a meaning that speaks most clearly to where you are in your life and circumstances. Jeffrey

Sumber, a clinical psychotherapist who studied global dream mythology at Harvard University, and Jungian dream interpretation at the Jung Institute in Zurich, has said that a dream could only be understood when the dreamer has an intimate knowledge of the self. In traditional, Jungian fashion, Sumber describes dreams as "bridge" which facilitates movement between our subconscious "knowing" and our conscious "belief about what we know". The conscious mind thinks it knows, but the subconscious mind is where the knowledge that, in truth, eludes us can readily be found and drawn out into our waking lives to inform and enrich them.

Sumber's statement points out how helpful a dream interpreter can be to understanding your dreams and what they mean to you. An interpreter can, with the assistance of some of the information in this book, set you on the path to being able to correctly interpret your own dreams. Discussing your dreams with a professional interpreter, you can begin to understand the shape dream analysis takes in the process of reading the meanings of your dreams in a systematic way. With the practice of dream analysis and interpretation you will come to know yourself better. There are some guidelines you can follow to make it easier for you to understand and analyze your dreams.

Maintain a record of your dreams
The first step in analyzing your dreams is to make note of them. Sumber says that when you write down your dreams, you are creating an image of the content of your subconscious mind; drawing it out and examining it. If you feel that you can't remember any given dream, keep a

journal by your bed and make a note saying 'No dreams to record'. You'll notice that within a span of two weeks, you will start remembering your dreams. The mere act of writing a negative record will train your mind to seek out the content of your dreams and to retain it more readily.

By keeping a record in the form of notes or a dream journal, you can maintain a log of what is essentially going on in your streaming subconscious mind. It is a bit like recording two lives: the life you live while you're awake and everything you're aware of in your waking experience, and a life in the layer beyond that, interpreted and generated from the activity in your subconscious. Dreaming and interpreting your dreams is a way of bridging the gap between the two worlds, so that you might gain a greater understanding of what is happening in your life and within you. Writing down your dreams on a consistent basis will have the effect of revealing trends that surface, about what's going on with you, over time. Maybe you are at a point in your life at which you feel more stress than usual. You may be choosing to go along with it, not knowing why, while trying to maintain some sense of peace.

With the aid of logging your dreams and their symbols, you may start to notice you're actually going through a period of internal growth, cleaning out old habits and emotions you've hung onto. It's a process. Over time, you'll see it doesn't last and that you are, in fact, transitioning to a new phase in your life - new projects, a new lifestyle or a new sense of self.

Identify the emotions in your dream

Ask yourself questions. Identify whether you were scared or remorseful or happy in the dream you've had. Did you experience those feelings only within the dream or are they still present when you wake up in the morning? In the case that emotions carry over from your dream to waking life, you should consider the possibility that this was an important dream, with great significance to you. This is because that it evoked such a strong and lasting emotional response from you. Being aware of that response means a better ability, on your part, to learn from your dreams about yourself, your motivations and how you can integrate that new insight into life improvements.

The reasons for dreams bringing something to your attention are myriad. There is no specific model when it comes to this. Dreams can help show you an aspect of yourself so that you can be more mindful of it, in future. They can also confirm an instinct you have had, or have only vaguely touched upon in your waking life. Dreams can help to reassure you of a current endeavor you're approaching so that you can proceed more confidently or more cautiously, whichever may be the case. They can also illuminate the need for you to take some time for meaningful introspection. Often, when we are experiencing blocks or obstacles in our waking lives, and can't seem to break through them, a dream may provide valuable insight as to what we can change in the way we usually go about it.

The final question should be whether or not you were comfortable with the feelings you encountered in the dream, itself. As you will probably have noticed from the interpretations listed in the common dreams section, a flying dream is mostly symbolic of a positive experience. Flying dreams primarily feature feelings of exhilaration, a joyous sense of freedom, being in control and surpassing challenges. But we also covered a variation on this theme that suggested you may not be ready for the next challenge. Why? Because in the context of dreams, an important factor is how you feel about the flying experience. When you are feeling afraid or uncomfortable, this changes the significance of the dream and its message from the subconscious. Similar differences can be seen in interpreting dreams about being naked, or witnessing your own death. If you experience these dreams without a sense of anxiety or fear (which are common emotional responses to these themes), a different interpretation may apply. Death and nudity dreams can have a positive message for you, as well as a negative one, as we've discussed in the section of common themes in dreams.

Identifying the elements of dreams
You are now beginning to notice (if you haven't already) that there is no concrete application when it comes to interpreting dreams. It is all circumstantial and subjective, in the same way the interpretation of events in the waking world is. That's why it's best to practice observing and remembering as much about your dream as you can, because every element can play a part in aligning the complete meaning of your dream for you.

As a character in your dream, you might appear in multiple ways. You will find a clear distinction between yourself and the different characters who may show up in the course of your dreams. You will have to understand your emotions toward these characters in your dreams, too. For example, you may show up in your dream as a certain actor or actress, from film or television. When interpreting your dreams, you will need to take into account how you feel about that actor or actress and what aspects or traits they model that you're either attracted to, or repelled by.

Cars as an element in your dream can have many different interpretations depending on a number of factors. First of all, is it a car, a truck, a semi-truck, or possibly a go-cart? Driving a car typically refers to your ambition, drive and your ability to navigate from one stage of life to another. What color is it painted? Are you the one driving the car, or are you in the passenger seat, or are you sitting in the back? If are the one driving, it signifies that you are the one in control of your life and directing where it's headed. It makes sense, right? If you are in the passenger's seat, you are taking a passive role. If you are in the back seat of the car, it shows you're either putting yourself down or allowing others to take over. This may point to a sense of low self-esteem or low self-confidence.

Then there are the conditions of the road to take into account. These usually associate linearly to your path and progress in your life. Is the road paved straight on or does it wind? Are you driving fast or moving slowly? Are you not moving at all, or parked somewhere? Have you lost your car, or has it been stolen? Have you flipped your car over? Have you driven your car into a body of water? Is it completely underwater? Have you hit someone with your car?

Hopefully you can see from this example that there are so many variations, even concerning one sole element of dreams (although a car is a particularly big one). All of these conditions and variations have specific meanings that will help you decipher more specifically what your dream is telling you. I hope you can take this example and apply the associations of variety to any other particular aspect or element of your dream. Don't worry. You don't have to do all this work by yourself. There are professional dream analysts who do this for a living who can help you sort out the elements of your dream.

If you are curious or interested in analyzing your dreams yourself, there are many websites and books about dream interpretation that you may find useful. Take a look at dreammoods.com, or buy their book, entitled *"What's in YOUR Dream?"* It is an A to Z volume of over 5,500 dream elements and their various meanings. When you use one of these websites or dream books to analyze, break your dream down element by element and discover their separate meanings. Once you have laid them all out in the order they appeared in your dream, you will start to notice one or several themes or trends emerging from these meanings. These themes will give you an overall sense of what the dream was about. The more you see a theme recurring, the more forcefully the dream is relaying that particular message to you.

There may be recurring elements in your dreams. Make note of these and pay close attention to them when interpreting your dream. These may be in the form of dream landscapes such as particular types of buildings or mountainsides. They can also be recurring objects, colors, numbers, and so on. As you continue to record your dreams, try to recall as many of these elements as you can. The most important ones are those that have stood out to you and bear the most significance. That goes to say that an element is significant if it triggers a sense of curiosity, out-of-place-ness, or a crazy or weird feeling. It's usually something that elicits an emotional or thought response, whether in the dream itself or afterward, when recalling the dream.

The fun thing about dreaming is that, usually, during the dream many things may seem commonplace, like flying for example. Once we recall the dream upon awakening, only then do we look at these things from the wakeful perspective that views them as very weird, or extraordinary.

You are the expert

Once you have a number of dreams written down, it's time to start interpreting them. Or you may prefer to interpret your dreams one by one, as they come to you. Whichever process you choose when starting out, you can use a dream dictionary to help you identify the meanings behind almost all the elements in your dream. Investigate reviews of the various dictionaries out there, as not all dream dictionaries are created equal. Choose one which acknowledges the various clinical and cultural threads of historical dream interpretation and choose one you feel provides the most comprehensive overview of dream symbolism. At the same time, keep in mind that you know yourself best and that your dreams are unique to you and you alone, regardless of any universal framework or symbols they may include.

Let your higher consciousness, self-knowledge and intuition guide you to learn how to understand and interpret your dreams. Stay open to allowing your dreams to tell you something about yourself that perhaps you were not aware of, or reluctant to look at in your waking life. You'll gain a lot of information about what's being transmitted to you from your subconscious. In so doing, you'll come to a fuller understanding of who you are, what makes you tick and areas you may have neglected that working on may prove beneficial.

Chapter 3: Nightmares

We've all had them; the jolt of terror as we run for our lives from some nameless and faceless horror. It's that jolt that brings us back to consciousness; back to the real world and the warm and cozy bed where we're safe. Nightmares happen all our lives, mostly beginning in childhood but why? And do we ever outgrow them?

This is a big topic and is highly person to the dreamer in question. What one person may consider a nightmare, another may have experience something considerably less disturbing. For example, somebody may have a dream involving zombies and feel terrified upon waking, drenched in a cold sweat. Another person could have a zombie dream and feel confident that they were able to vanquish the zombies, or see it as little more than a reflection of a movie they'd watched the night before. Conversely, a person could dream about a ghost and feel comfortable, based on the nature of the dream and the ghost's presence. Another person could have a similar dream, in which a ghost may have been harmless. But because it represented a deep underlying fear transmitted from their subconscious, they might feel deeply disturbed upon waking from it.

Another example of the subjective nature of the scary images in dreams can be as follows. You may have a dream where you are witnessing pigs having their heads cut off and blood spraying in every direction. You might see the pigs dismembered and disemboweled and never having witnessed anything like what's occurring in the dream (or perhaps only having seen something similar in a horror movie) awaken terrified and alarmed. Then again, in the case of a butcher or someone who works in a slaughterhouse, the dream may resemble an average day at the abattoir. Perhaps all the butcher may feel is that work is a bit much at the moment, as it's crossing over into the land of dreams.

In general, nightmares are caused by a tremendous amount of stress and anxiety in your waking life. It is difficult to process all of these emotions, especially if they're prevalent day after day. The nightmares you may have because of these emotions are a way for your subconscious to sort through your stress without you having to experience complete nervous breakdown. Often this doesn't help, as nightmares prevent you from getting a good night's rest, especially if you wake up from one in the middle of the night and are unable to get back to sleep because of it.

You may also have a nightmare because of the way in which a certain dream element taps into your fears. Monsters, zombies, ghosts, vampires, aliens - all these can represent highly personal fears. It's usually the case that when you wake up from a terrifying dream involving one or more of these elements, you begin to experience irrational fear for yourself or loved ones. You may give in to the fear that there's something horrifying lurking in

your home similar to what you saw in the dream. Have you
ever actually had something like that happen after waking
up from a nightmare? Probably not. Your nightmares
aren't real, except in the sense that they work out fears in
your subconscious you may be unaware of, while awake.

In popular culture, films about monsters like the ones
listed above, as well as those about serial killers, serve the
purpose of providing a locus for communal fear. These
monsters represent, in a safe setting, those things we
genuinely fear in life. The vampire might be the blood
sucking corporate raider. The werewolf, the sexual
predator. By giving faces to some of our most pressing
fears and anxieties, these filmic creatures serve us by
presenting themselves as mythical embodiments of those
things we most ardently fear. They allow us to get a good
look them. While we can't do much about them, for the
most part, we can watch the film's protagonist drive a
stake through their hearts, or perhaps shoot them with
silver bullets. Watching the Walking Dead, for example,
gives a lot of people the satisfaction of seeing the heads of
zombies explode, or be lopped off. These scenes of
monsters being destroyed is a type of surrogacy for our
desire to defeat and destroy unsavory societal influences
beyond our control, as well as to conquer our own,
personal demons.

But sometimes these films about the embodiment of our
fears in mythical monster form are the very sources of our
most frightening nightmares. The emotions and fear you
had experience while watching such films can be

transported into your dreams. This is why external circumstances that bring about certain emotional responses in you, can sometimes have a deep impact on the nature of your dreams. These external circumstances are real and can make our dreams seem equally real. If the nature of the dream is dark, violent, or frightening, the effect can be profound – and seem very real. Even if it's a movie, we've seen it with our own eyes. The imagery has penetrated to the deepest layer of our subconscious and can bring forth some unwelcome fruit, in the form of nightmares.

Nightmares are so scary because they bring to the surface your fears, whether you are aware of them, or they're tuck away in the deep recesses of your mind. This subcategory of dreams may be a method for your unconscious to command your attention, provoking it to examine a situation or problem you may have been avoiding. It could also be a warning about your health, or another circumstance that requires your urgent attention. Some studies have shown that people who are more prone to having nightmares tend to be more sensitive, intuitive, creative, or imaginative in nature. It's possible that this is because they're more empathetic and in tune to their environment. MORE ON THIS

Even though they're scary, our dream lives are a safe place for our nightmares to come out to play and work out the fears they represent. You don't have to go into the middle of the woods at night and conjure up the boogieman to face your personal fears. You can do it (and you may well have been doing it already, to your discomfort) in your own dream space. Fears represent what is unknown, and once we come to know the, we can get them under control and master them.

Consider walking through a dark and cluttered room and the eerie feeling you get as your imagination plays tricks with you. Tricks with light. Tricks with shadows. Tricks with past experiences of your fear of the darkness. If someone suddenly turns the light on in this room, so that every corner is illuminated, the fear vanishes. Now, perhaps the only thought you're having is that it's time for a garage sale. The only fear, that you may be a hoarder.

One effective way to reduce the occurrence of nightmares is by writing down what you can remember about them as soon as you wake up. This will help you release some of the emotions associated with them and set the foundation for you to analyze them, later on. Analyzing and discussing your nightmares with others will help you get to the bottom of their underlying meanings. Once you generate an understanding of the nature of your nightmares and the issues they highlight, you will know how to confront the problem. You will be able to slowly work toward resolving it and reducing the influence of the fears your nightmares represent.

Why Nightmares Happen

Nightmares can be vivid and they can be frightening. Their imagery that can leave you waking in panic and fear, with your heart pounding. Nearly all young children experience nightmares, and between the ages of 5 and 12, up to 50% of those nightmares will be strong enough to disturb their parents, as well, due to children waking up from them crying and screaming. Children's nightmares can stem from a number of sources – a scary story, watching a scary show on TV, or even felling stressed and anxious about something. While most kids eventually grow out of nightmares, not all do. The nightmares linger on into adulthood.

Around 2 to 8% of the adult population suffers from nightmares and some of these are triggered by the same sources as children's nightmares. It is important to understand that a dream, even a nightmare, is a thinking process - a combination of the thoughts that stream through your mind all day. Nightmares happen when difficult thoughts and issues run through our minds, and our subconscious seeks to deal with them, during REM sleep. During the day, we tend to put difficulties to one side ignore them, but at night we can't do that. At night, we are alone with our thoughts and the difficulties need to be addressed.

However, bad or difficult thoughts are not the only reason we have nightmares. A poor diet can also contribute to how frequently we experience these episodes. Some people will experience a nightmare after eating something late at night (cheese is notorious) that may exacerbate the tendency. Foods high carbohydrates tend to increase activity in the brain and raise metabolism, so eating them late at night is a recipe for a nightmare.

Adult nightmares are spontaneous but usually triggered by depression, anxiety or poor nutrition, which all contribute to other psychological factors. If you suffer from a chronic sleep disorder, such as sleep apnea or restless leg syndrome, you may also be more likely to suffer recurrent nightmares. So, what is happening in the brain when these nightmares happen?

The Brain and Nightmares

Nightmares usually occur during the last few hours of the night, a time when REM sleep is at its peak. I will describe this in greater detail in the next chapter, but the sleep cycle is split into four separate stages. Sleep onset, light sleep, and two stages of deep sleep, one of which is the REM stage. REM sleep actually occurs around every 90 minutes, throughout the night and it is at this time our brains are at their most active. Dreaming will actually happen in all the sleep stages. Approximately 80% of people will wake during the first two stages, while around 40% will be awakened from deep cycle sleep by their dreams.

The culprit appears to be the amygdala, which is regulated by the frontal lobes. Neuroimaging studies have shown that the amygdala is in a highly active state during REM and it is this part of the brain that handles negative emotions, which goes some way towards explaining why some people have nightmares.

Dreamers Who Have Nightmares

While young children are more susceptible to nightmares and only a small percentage of adults occasionally have them, some are more prone to them than others. A number of studies have determined that three things can have an influence on how often dreamers have nightmares – personality type, age and trauma. A study published in 1990 found that 47% of college students suffered at least one nightmare during the two-week study period. None of these nightmares were linked with anxiety, which suggested that nightmares are perhaps more common in young adults than was previously believed.

Other studies showed that everyday fears, like being involved in a car accident, could trigger nightmares in blind people. In fact, in 2014 a study was published which found that blind people would experience up to four times more nightmares than those who could see. That study confirmed that there was a link between emotions that were experienced by blind people during waking hours; situations that had the potential to be embarrassing like spilling coffee everywhere and the incidence of nightmares.

Past traumas and certain personality types also played a large role in the occurrence and recurrence of nightmares. People who are sensitive, who avoid confrontation whenever possible, and who find themselves let down more often than others, are prone to having nightmares, because life is somewhat more difficult for them.

The Dark Truth Behind the Nightmare

As with dreams, there are common symbols in nightmares, like murder or death. Death nightmares usually signify that something has or is about to change (or end). Dreams about death involving children usually happen when a child has reached a major milestone (learning how to walk or talk, the first day at school or passing a driving test). Dreams about your own child dying are usually caused by the realization, sometimes difficult, that time is passing quickly and the baby running around in diapers while "die", to be replaced by a more independent child, or young adult.

In a similar way, dreams about murder are also about change or something ending, but usually with an ending that is forced. We dream that someone is trying to murder us when we are under pressure to change something or end it. Nightmares like this can be about us personally, or about something in our lives. It could be a relationship that has ended, or needs to end. The situation may even be a pregnancy because pregnancies force significant behavioral changes.

Nightmares can also be linked to events occurring many years before. In one study, a participant who was in a happy, secure marriage began having terrible nightmares in which she was being brutally attacked during a war. She would sometimes dream that her husband had left her alone in a dark parking lot overnight. It came to light that she had been abused as a child and made to feel as though she wasn't wanted. She was never helped, at the time of the abuse and learned to suppress the feelings and the memories as they arose, as a type of psychological defense. Conflicts that have not been resolved do not just disappear. They play an important part in forming the people we become and our personalities. Events in our childhoods can lead to insecurity in adulthood and continual validation-seeking. It can lead to all criticism being seen as a personal attack. Our life experiences, especially those which occur in childhood, deeply influence our lives and also, our dreams.

Chapter 4: Sleep Stages

In order to get a better idea of how and when dreams occur, it's helpful to know about the human brain's typical sleep patterns. These are also known as sleep cycles or sleep stages. Understanding the nature of each stage and the varying brain wave function during each is the basis of how scientists and psychologists are able to conduct dream studies in the laboratory.

This information will show you where dreams occur in your sleep cycle. With this knowledge, you can plan your sleep schedule in order to plan when to wake up so you are more likely to remember a dream. You will also be able to set the right environment for increasing your chances of having a lucid dream and to employ the techniques that can help you create one. These will be described in the next chapter. Knowing how a sleep cycle works also provides valuable information about how to return to sleep, should you wake up in the middle of the night because of a dream. You will learn how it's possible to easily go back to sleep. The sleep stages and their characteristics are outlined for you here with as much technical jargon cut out as possible, while explanations of essential technicalities are provided for you.

There are five stages you go through while sleeping, which are aptly categorized in roman numerals as stages I through IV, with the fifth and final one known as REM, or Rapid Eye Movement sleep. Each stage involves varying levels of eye movement and breathing patterns, as well as brain wave patterns. An interesting note, as you may have experienced at some point in your life, is that when a person first falls asleep, he or she does not always begin in stage I. This depends individual levels of both physical and intellectual activity during the day and duration of wakefulness. For example, those of you who are used to burning the candle at both ends, may find you enter into a deep sleep as soon as you lay down. In cases of extreme exhaustion (as experienced by shift workers, students or workaholics), deep, dream stage sleep may be reached almost immediately. Those who spend a lot of time exercising their brains, only catching small periods of sleep of 30 minutes to several hours between work sessions are more prone to this organization of the sleep cycle.

- *Stage I*: This is the beginning of the sleep cycle and the typical starting point for someone falling sleep. Stage I sleep can be characterized as a state of semi-consciousness in which one might be easily be awakened. In this light sleep, eye movement is slow, and the feeling that one is starting to fall asleep occurs. This is also where beta waves are still present, but beginning to decrease. Beta waves are the fastest of all the brain waves we typically operate under throughout the day, to process high volumes of information. Alpha waves, which are a bit slower than beta waves, increase in activity during this stage.

- *Stage II*: The eyes stop moving in this stage. Alpha wave activity becomes more predominant and encourages deeper rest and relaxation. Beta waves continue to decrease in activity, but still show occasional bursts of activity called sleep spindles.

- *Stage III*: Brain waves are much slower in this stage. Beta wave function reduces to the background, while alpha and theta waves (which are slower still than alpha) are running the show. Theta waves are believed to link the conscious and subconscious minds. Brain wave studies have also shown that devout practitioners of deep meditation such as Yogis and Buddhist monks have an increase in their theta wave activity, both during meditation and while awake. Delta waves, characteristic of a deep-sleep pattern, are intermixed here as well.

- *Stage IV*: Only delta waves are emitted from the brain during this time. This is the deepest state of sleep and is linked to an unconscious state of mind. People who sleep like bears are very familiar with this state, not being disturbed by any moderate kind of stimulation, with the exception of very loud and abrupt noises or being physically shaken awake. This stage is extremely important because it's when the body secretes hormones that enable new growth for children and adolescents, and repair and regeneration in the bodies of adults. If you are constantly feeling achy or fatigued, it is most likely

because your quality of sleep is suffering and you're
not spending enough sleep time, if any, in stage IV.

- *REM Sleep*: Breathing in this stage is shallow,
  rapid, and irregular. As the name suggests, eye
  movement behind the closed lids is very rapid, also.
  Muscular activity elsewhere in the body, like the
  limbs, is usually absent. Heart rate and blood
  pressure approach waking levels. This is also the
  stage in which dreams occur. Alpha and theta waves
  become more present again, however it is the alpha
  waves which are most common in REM sleep.

Over the course of the night's sleep, people cycle through
each of the five stages and then start over again, at Stage I.
It takes about 90 to 100 minutes to complete a sleep cycle,
although the amount of time spent in each stage varies,
according to the time of night. In other words, a person
spends more time in stages III and IV at the beginning of
the night and most time in stage I and REM sleep toward
the morning. Overall a healthy balance of sleep stages
allows an adult to spend 20% to 25% of the night's sleep in
REM stage, 50% of the time in Stage II, and 30% of the
time in the other stages.

Given the amount of time it takes to complete a sleep cycle,
you can generally time your sleep schedule to allow you to
wake up right around the cusp of the REM stage of sleep.
This practice will allow you a better chance of
remembering your dreams if you feel you don't typically
have any. In the event you usually find yourself at a loss to

remember the details of your dreams, you'll be more likely to remember then if you do this. For example, if you plan to go to sleep at 10 pm, you can set an alarm for around 4 o'clock in the morning, 5:30, 7 o'clock or 8:30 to catch yourself in the REM stage. You have to count out and plan the amount of time which will elapse between when you go to sleep and the commencement of the first cycle. After that, each of the cycles should be accounted for at a duration of between 90 and 100 minutes. You'll read about how psychologists do this in dream laboratories in the next chapter on lucid dreaming. If you do not succeed at first in trying this experiment, give it time and keep trying. The more you try, the more you increase your chances of catching a dream, documenting it and analyzing its contents.

In a related matter, you may wake up from a dream in the middle of the night, disturbing your sleep. You may have a difficult time getting back to sleep, depending on the nature of you regular sleep schedule, how much stress you're under, and the nature of the dream you've had. If this is the case, it helps to get something of it out.

Keep a journal next to your bed so you can write what you remember about your dream immediately. Writing it down will allow you to review it later so you don't have to sit up at night, running the dream through your head and wondering about it. Likewise, if the dream evoked a strong emotional response from you, writing it down will make it a lot easier to release those feelings instead of allowing them to stew inside you, preventing your return to sleep.

If thoughts arise like, "Oh great, now that I'm up I'll never get back to sleep again," remember: you have just come out of the last stage of your sleep cycle. That means you'll naturally feel more awake and your body may think it's time to get up. Your brain is on the cusp of beta wave mode – fast-functioning, busy information processing. And if it does not have any food it will find its own, digging up old concerns or backlogged information on your schedule and to-do lists, so that it will have something to process. This is primarily why you have trouble getting back to sleep. You can trick your brain when this happens.

Having just emerged from the end of one sleep cycle, so how can you fluidly slip back into the next one? Sit up in your bed for a moment. Begin breathing moderately to deeply at a rhythmic pace. Remember that REM sleep causes shallow, rapid breathing, so your body and brain have lower levels of oxygen. That factor can prevent you from being adequately relaxed. This is part of the natural mechanism that allows you to wake up in the first place.

Once you have found a steady and comfortable breathing pace for a minute or two, slowly stand. Keep the pace of breathing steady and do a few simple stretches. Raise your arms over your head for a good stretch, do a forward bend and try to touch your toes, etc. Your brain activity will settle' a bit because it will think that you are getting ready for the day. So far, you will have somewhat evaded the effect of your brain's natural tendency to return to full wakefulness. Now take in the darkness of the room with your eyes. Soften your gaze and tell yourself that it is still night and tell yourself you're going back to sleep. Take a look at your bed and make a mental note of how inviting it appears. Keep breathing deeply and steadily and climb back into bed. Settle into the feeling of comfort you get from being under the sheets and blanket and nestling into your pillow. Tell yourself you're going back to sleep again and close your eyes. Focus on the deep, relaxing breaths you're taking. Soon, you should be able to slip back into the semi-consciousness of Stage I sleep.

Something else to know about dreaming is that it can be work. You may have gotten a sense of this notion from reading about the emotional processing, memory sorting, and problem solving nature of dreams in the previous chapters of this book. There may have been times you've woken up feeling exhausted and wondering why, when supposedly you've enjoyed a full night's sleep. You may logically believe you feel this way because of working so hard the previous day or week, or because you're going through a period of stress. These reasons may well be valid, to a degree. Dreams may serve to help process these reasons, but that means you're working while you sleep too. This effect truly defines the expression "burning the candle at both ends".

Anyone who has endured working through an emotional problem knows it can be quite exhausting. The same goes for trying to work through a vast amount of information to bring order and coherence to it. Since dreams can potentially assist in doing this work for you while you sleep, they can also contribute to a feeling of exhaustion the next day. This usually happens when you have a lot going on in your life and feel as though you have too many balls in the air. A way to prevent this from happening is to make yourself open to suggestion.

Make it a practice when you go to bed each night to make some affirmations. The more you're able to convince yourself of these declarations, while trusting and believing in them, the more helpful they'll be. Make a game of it – the more fun you're having, the more you allow yourself to open up to the practice of self-affirmation. You have absolutely nothing to lose by experimenting with this practice and everything to gain.

Next, as you're lying in bed about to fall asleep, tell yourself, "I may allow myself the time to dream, but it cannot take away from my restful sleep." You can also say, "I will wake up feeling rested and fresh, ready to take on the day." Believe in these words, and repeat them to yourself as necessary until you feel you can trust that this is what's going to happen. A lot depends on your conviction while saying them. Believing in your ability to make it happen is half the battle. But don't try too hard. That can get you worked up and that's the last thing you want to be when attempting to go back to sleep.

You can tell yourself you have a vacation coming up and you're going to enjoy yourself. You believe it because you have set up a belief structure around the idea of what a vacation means to you: it promotes rest, relaxation, and fun. And when you truly believe in something, it usually follows that it becomes reality. Make returning to the first stage of the sleep your reality. Believe that's where you're headed and remind yourself that's what you believe will happen with affirmations. Keep practicing. The more consistent you are, the faster you'll notice results. Sleep well, and see you in the next chapter.

Chapter 5: Lucid Dreaming

Have you ever dreamed you were an astronaut or a bird? Have you dreamed that you were soaring through the clouds and shooting across the sky like Superman? Have you imagined a vacation on a Caribbean island? Did you find it any less enjoyable because it was a dream? You enjoyed every bit of your dream, regardless of whether it was only your subconscious soaring through the sky, or basking in the Caribbean sun. What if you could will yourself to dream of such pleasant, uplifting things?

As mentioned in earlier chapters, lucid dreaming is a state in which you're aware you're dreaming. Lucid dreaming can help us fully exercise the power of our personal dream world. We're able to change the direction of our dreams and also to change the objects and characters in them. For instance, if you are in a lucid dream, and your environment is your bedroom, you can make your bed fly. You can create an entirely different universe behind the door to your bedroom. It's like writing your very own comic book, romance novel or action film. It has been proven that lucid dreams exist. There are many techniques you can use to begin mastering the art of lucid dreaming, which will cover shortly, but let's take a look at theories around lucid dreaming.

As mentioned earlier in this book, the idea of lucid dreaming was first examined and named in 1912 by the Dutch psychiatrist, Frederik Willem van Eeden. But even before that time, the 1867 book by Marquis d'Hervey de

Saint-Denys, *Dreams and the ways to Direct them: Practical Observations*, discussed lucid dreaming in depth. The book marks the first instance of the use of the term "lucid dreaming" and is the West's seminal work in lucid dream research. So, almost 50 years before van Eeden, Saint-Denys named the phenomenon and researched it.

While Saint-Denys work on the subject uses the term in a less clinically informed way than we use it today, the phrase "lucid dreaming" is employed many times throughout the book. Further, his use of the term does not refer directly to what we now call lucid dreaming. Rather it refers to the state experienced directly before a lucid dream begins, noting the clarity of content, in terms of images and the realistic nature of the dream. Yet, Saint-Denys expressly writes of being "aware" in the context of his dreams, as well as the ability to guide their directions and outcomes. That is, indeed, the modern definition of lucid dreaming. Herein lies the ambiguity of his thought, as he appears in his work, to be exploring rather than expounding, as the later Van Eeden did.

Van Eeden's research into lucid dreams was certainly influenced by Saint-Denys, whose influence extends to researchers who followed, including Dr. Celia Greene. In Van Eeden's work, *A Study of Dreams*, he expressly mentions Saint-Denys. Specifically, Van Eeden's complaints about having his assertions concerning conscious dreaming dismissed by other researchers encompass Saint-Denys, who he claims to have been met with similar dismissal by others in the field of dream interpretation.

But lucid dreaming has many proponents in modern times, building on the work of Saint-Denys and van Eeden. Despite many clinicians' tendency to discard its finding as empirically unsound, it's clear that many people all over the world, experience lucid dreaming. All the same, science on the subject is inconclusive, at best.

A 2012 study which appeared in the Journal Consciousness and Cognition (Induction of Lucid Dreams: A Systematic Review and Evidence), was actually a conglomeration of 35 separate studies, conducted in both sleep laboratories and the field. The study found that the induction techniques employed were inconsistent and unreliable. However, it also found that some of them were promising. This prompted study authors to recommend that further study, arising from their findings, be pursued. Recently, though, researchers have begun to study subjects who can reliably induce lucid dreams via their own methodology and are studying human consciousness within the context of these people's dreams.

The study employs a technique uncovered by dream researchers Stephen LaBerge and Keith Hearne. Participants (known to reliably and regularly induce lucid dreams) are able to signal researchers when they've started dreaming, via a series of eye movements. These are discussed with the research team prior to the participant's going to sleep, in order that they not be mistaken for the normal eye movements associated with REM sleep. Electronic equipment is used to verify the movements and their nature, in order to ensure that they're not involuntary but that they fit the pre-arranged criteria.

These neuroscientific studies have revealed distinctive brain activity present in those experiencing lucid dreams which is nothing like either that seen during the REM cycle, or in the waking brain. This has provided many who know lucid dreaming is real and not just a cherished wish, with hope for further research toward solid empirical evidence.

Swiss neuroscientist, Daniel Erlacher has taken the findings of Hearne and LaBerge one step further. His research involves "in dream" studies which require participants to perform activities found in normal life, while dreaming. Using the same eye movement protocol to signal that lucid dreaming is taking place, Erlacher asked participants to signal when they were performing the activities prescribed. His research discovered that the amount of time it takes us to perform these activities (for example, counting) in waking life, is the same amount required in the context of a lucid dream. This research takes us one important step closer to proving, once and for all, that lucid dreaming is a real thing and a portal to understanding the interaction between our waking and sleeping minds. But lucid dreaming has some very practical applications, which we'll review now.

A practical use of lucid dreaming is emphasized in the following story. There was a woman who once had a dream she was walking in a swamp in the day time and arrived at the edge of a pond. When she drew near the bank, an alligator appeared and began to chase her. Turning away, she ran in fear, feeling her life threatened. She then realized she was dreaming. Once she realized this, she again turned around and confronted the alligator. She asked it why it was chasing her. Without a word, the alligator began to emit a putrid smell and fumes arose from all around it. Then, before her eyes, it transformed into a pile of smoldering cigarette butts. On waking the woman realized that the dream was a message from her subconscious that she should quit smoking, because of the danger her habit represented to health.

As you can see from this example, this woman used the power of lucid dreaming to confront the object of her fear – the alligator – once she realized she was dreaming and that no harm could come to her. When she was able to do that, the object transformed into something more meaningful that applied to her daily life. She was able to elicit a pure and direct message because of being able to manipulate her dream. In turn, she was able transform her dream into something that would benefit her waking life. Such is the power of learning to use lucid dreams to your advantage.

Lucid dreaming is a unique experience. It's also a very good way to recall your dreams. Lucid dreams help you interpret your dreams effectively, because you are aware of what is going on in the dream. You can create your own stage in your dreams to rehearse for a confrontation you know is coming, the following day. Lucid dreams help you become more self-confident and can have the effect of making you more willing to confront threats. This form of dreaming can also help you train for something coming up in your waking life. Many athletes make their technique seem completely effortless because they have visualized their performance countless times beforehand, in their minds. They rehearse their movements and picture themselves being successful, so that when the time comes to perform, it's much easier for them to win. This is usually done while they are conscious, but some athletes who are able to dream lucidly will practicing their moves in basketball, tennis, or marathon running.

Lucid dreams are a form of auto-mind control which follows ideas propounded by Law of Attraction, as popularized in the 2006 book *The Secret*. The principles of the Law of Attraction teach people to bring into their lives what they truly desire. It's also a method for overcoming fears and anxieties, by learning to control and excise negative thinking. You can purposely put yourself in a situation in your dream in which you know it's a safe place to rehearse such circumstances and confront what you feel intimidates you in real life. By practicing this in your dream space, you will ingrain positive outcomes in your mind for a time when such circumstances arise again in your waking life. By that time, you'll feel prepared to take them on.

You can use lucid dreams to ask for a raise at work, prepare for a first date, overcome personal phobias and get over any kind of block you're having, whether it is creative, professional, or romantic. Because brain activity during the dream state is similar to the kind of activity present during a waking life event, what you "learn" or "practice" provides you the same kind of training as you'd have if you were awake. You are effectively hardwiring your brain and are only limited by the extent of your imagination. With practice, you can learn how to elicit a lucid dream at will.

Techniques for Lucid Dreaming

There have been many techniques developed to assist people in having lucid dreams. This section covers those techniques. All have been approved by psychologists, with some endorsed by professional dream analysts.

WBTB

WBTB is an acronym for '*Wake – Back – To – Bed*'. The method is very simple. It is more effective, however, when combined with another technique, known as MILD (see below). The MILD/WBTB combination is by far the best used to enhance lucid dreaming. Once you've gone to bed, set an alarm to wake yourself up, after four hours of sleep. Plan to add on the time it takes for you to typically fall asleep. Then keep yourself awake for an hour or less. You can read about lucid dreaming for that one hour. That way, you are sending a signal to your brain that you're ready to enjoy a lucid dream. This is not necessary, after the first few times. This technique is best for those who are interested in strengthening other techniques, like MILD.

MILD

MILD is an acronym for '*Mnemonic Induction of Lucid Dreams*'. The MILD technique works best when combined with WBTB.

This process requires a lot of concentration on your part. Before you go to sleep, repeat a mantra to yourself. This mantra must be along the lines of '*I know I am dreaming.*' You have to remind yourself that you will know you are dreaming, once asleep. If this doesn't help, visualize yourself in a dream. Assume the dream is about you shooting across the sky like a comet. Tell yourself you KNOW that you're flying across the sky like a comet. Repeat this vision to yourself until you're sure it has fixed itself in your mind, or until you fall asleep.

You can also try a counting method to enter a lucid state. When you are in bed ready to sleep, start counting to yourself while repeating the mantra afterward, "One, I am dreaming. Two, I am dreaming, Three, I am dreaming..." After a certain amount of time you will be counting "Sixty-one, I am dreaming," and by that time you really will be. It is a good idea to try this method when you are already tired and ready for sleep. If you try this while your mind is racing or when you're still wide awake, you may end up keeping yourself awake instead. On the other hand, if counting sheep has worked for you before, counting yourself into a lucid dream will certainly be effective.

If you're having difficulty mastering the technique, you can tell yourself to wake up right after a dream or use the

WBTB technique. Once you're awake, if you've had a dream, you can make note of it in your journal and read it. Then visualize the dream and tell yourself you know that you were dreaming. This way, you'll be able to ensure you're having a lucid dream. This technique is best for people who have a good idea about how to pursue sustained visualization, but visualization is something anyone can learn to do.

Used by people all over the world as a support for work, sports, dance and other forms of art, visualization is a technique that allows us to see ourselves attaining a goal, or performing a task in the way we wish to replicate it in the normal course of our lives. Professional athletes use visualization extensively. Dancers also use this technique, especially when choreographing dance routines to music. They literally train their minds to envision the movements that sync with the music and most eloquently express it.

The trick is to allow yourself to see a sustained and detailed vision of your accomplishment of a task, or a goal. Step by step, taking you through the process of doing whatever it is you want to get done, you see in your mind's eye what you need to physically replicate in order to complete the task or achieve the goal. This is essentially an intellectual exercise that sends your body the message that the task at hand is doable; the goal, achievable. Walking your mind through the steps invests your body with the ability to perform them. The same is true of lucid dreaming. If you are able to concentrate on the desired goal, visualizing all it entails in as much detail as possible, the message is that it's achievable. You are telling yourself you can do it, as though watching a "how to" video.

Autosuggestion

This technique has been used in scientific research and has proved to be highly effective. It works best for people who are susceptible to hypnosis. If you are someone who is open to suggestion, you will likely be successful with this technique.

Before you sleep, repeat to yourself that you will have a lucid dream. Keep chanting this to yourself. Believe in what you're and make sure you're aware of what you're expecting from a lucid dream is. It's important to understand that, while you can move yourself toward lucid dreaming, it's not something you can force. Believing that you will have a lucid dream makes having one more likely. Let yourself genuinely believe that you will have a lucid dream. Don't try too hard. It might take some time for you to arrive at the point where you're able to enjoy a lucid dream, or even to have such dreams on a regular basis. With consistent practice in training your mind, as well as an attitude of settling into a state of relaxation as part of the process, you'll improve the likelihood of lucid dreaming.

This method can also be used to recall your dreams. Before you go to sleep, tell yourself you will remember your dreams. It's important to remember that these things can't be forced. They can only be fostered or encouraged. Although this method is very effective, it doesn't work for everybody. It only has a chance of working, in fact, when you're calm, relaxed and believe you have the capability to dream lucidly. Meditation can also help you prepare your mind for approaching lucid dreaming by calming your mind and body, as you prepare for sleep.

Is This a Dream?

Throughout your waking day, periodically ask yourself, "Is this a dream?" especially if something odd happens. It will be helpful if you avoid making this a rhetorical question. Pose the question to yourself seriously and then take a moment to consider it. The trick is not to dispel the wonder or mystery by answering immediately with a dismissive responsive, like, "Of course I am not dreaming!"

A good way to check in with yourself is to look at something that provides you with real world information. For example, you can glance at a clock or a watch and then check it a second time. If you are dreaming, the time will always change dramatically when you look at it the second time. If y reading something, whether at home, at work, or in the street, look away and then read it again. If you're dreaming, whatever you have been reading will be totally different at second glance.

You must do this often enough that it becomes a habit, so start out with 10 to 15 times per day. With your brain trained to ask this question and to go through the motions of ensuring you're not dreaming, the habit of questioning your state of wakefulness will induce the question to appear automatically in your dreams, and you will be on your way to dreaming lucidly.

Using Signals

Signals refer to objects, images, or actions in your dream that provide cues to let you know you're dreaming. Basically, you can use anything as a signal and it will be unique to you as an individual. Read through the notes you've taken on your dreams or go back through your dream journal to identify something that frequently appears in your dreams. By choosing a recurring image, you have a better chance of seeing it in a future dream. When you're ready to go to sleep, tell yourself "When I see my old house, I'll know I'm dreaming". This is just one example of a signal. You can use any recurring image from past dreams. The same goes for odd occurrences in your dreams. If you find yourself flying or breathing underwater frequently, don't ignore it. Instead let it be a sign that you are dreaming, using it as a signal to indicate to your sleeping mind that you are not in a wakeful, but a sleeping state.

The Hypnagogic State: How to Have Lucid Dreams Using Hypnagogia

The hypnagogic state is a sensory experience that marks the point at which you're about to fall asleep. It is almost certain you'll be aware of it, even if you've never given it any thought or paid attention to it in the past. It's a mild hallucinogenic state that may be used by people to experience semi-wakeful lucid dreaming, remaining fully aware of them as they fall asleep. In a hypnagogic state, you can also shape your dreams as you wish.

"Only when I am on the brink of sleep, with the consciousness that I am so..."

\- Edgar Allan Poe

What is The Hypnagogic State?

Hypnagogia includes a somewhat mesmerizing range of sounds, visions, sensations and insights as you traverse the boundary of the sleep-wake state. It will normally start with something called phosphenes, which are rather vague purple and green blobs. They will appear a little luminescent on the backs of your eyelid when your eyes are closed.

These little blobs will eventually turn into something more interesting, gradually changing to landscapes and faces that are more familiar. The deeper into a hypnagogic state you go, without falling asleep, the more likely hallucinations are – sounds like voices and music. This is the beginning of the dream state.

The patterns that flow across your vision are complex and become more so as they move. You will be drawn into a hypnagogic hypnotic state, which you can manipulate as you wish. What many people do not realize is that, when they experience this, the images can lead to lucid dreams.

The hypnagogic state is not limited to visuals either. You can also experience auditory hypnagogia, hearing normal sounds like a phone ringing, music playing, or someone calling your name. Hypnagogia can actually make you feel as though you're floating above your body.

What Causes Hypnagogia?

Some people consider it to be activity in the brain that has no meaning, just a way of clearing out junk that is no longer needed. Others say hypnagogia has more value than that.

In a similar way to lucid dreaming, hypnagogia can be guided and interpreted consciously, as it happens, cementing a communication with the unconscious that is two-way. Scientists say that the hypnagogic state is linked to four different stages of sleep NREM, REM, pre-sleep alpha wave and relaxed wakefulness. There is also a theory that meditating on a regular basis can help you develop skills that let you freeze the hypnagogic state later and later throughout the process.

Hypnagogic Exercise Number 1

Although it's generally experienced just before sleep, there is a way for you to experience a little mild hypnagogia while you are wide awake, and mentally alert.

- Shut your eyes and cup your hands over the eye sockets without touching the eyeballs.
- Focus somewhere on the middle distance – what do you see?
- You might see, to start with, an image burned from the glare of your screen but these will evolve into very faint visual images, something like a holographic wallpaper over your eyelids
- These will appear as geometric patterns, static ones that intensify a little when you focus directly on them

Hypnagogic Exercise Number 2

- Start off by lying in a quiet dark room, just as you would if you were going to sleep.
- Allow your eyes to naturally close and just observe the darkness around you.
- Relax as deeply as you can and try to convince your body that you're going to go to sleep*.
  - The real challenge here is quietening your mind enough to silence the mind chatter while holding on to a small sliver of awareness.
  - You should begin to see some amorphous blobs of color, slowly moving their way through your field of vision.
- They will begin to take shape as something a little more interesting and, at this point, you can will them to take the shape of whatever you want to see. Tell yourself what you want to see and then look for it.

- As you become more adept at doing this, you will be able to evolve these shapes i and people into place and this will dictate what your upcoming lucid dream will be about.
- At some point in the process, your dreaming mind will take the reins, and will begin to introduce new visuals, just beyond the field of your vision.
- You should experience sensations, visual recall and emotions from beyond the projected images.
- At this point, the lucid dream will begin.
- If you can stay aware, you will be in a lucid dream. To be truly WILD there must be no lapse in consciousness, only a few moments of loss of awareness. You will then remember you are dreaming.
- Depending on the state of mind and relaxation you're in when the hypnagogic state starts, it can take anywhere from a few seconds to half an hour for the state to turn into a lucid dream.
- At this stage, it's your call as to whether you continue or, stop. If you feel restless, it's probably time to stop, but if you feel sleepy and dreamy, then carry on if you want to.

* A better time to start this would be when you awake in the night, after you have had several hours sleep and are already highly relaxed.

This technique for hypnagogic induction is a great way of exploring the realms that exist between wakefulness and sleep. You will find you can be deeply relaxed, have some pretty trippy visuals, your thoughts will be clear, your stress will be gone and you will gain some new insights.

Some people find this difficult to get the hang of to start with, but the hardest part is moving from the hypnagogic state to a state of lucid dreaming in which you are deeply engaged. It's worth practicing, though, because this is also seen as a very powerful form of meditation.

Some Amazing Benefits of Lucid Dreaming

While it can be great fun to make your escape from life into a lucid dream, the real benefits of lucid dreaming go much, much deeper. The experience is full engrossing. It is an explosion in your senses and an alternative reality in which you can live a life free of worry and stress, without fear or inhibitions, and with the confidence that you can do exactly what you want.

This is a liberation that can have a real impact on your waking life. But, wait a minute; dreams can't possibly have any effect on real life, can they? I mean, the effects of a fantastic lucid dream are going to wear off eventually. But I'm about to share with you twelve of the most amazing benefits of lucid dreaming, both while you're awake and sleeping, and I will give you some real world examples (without naming any names) that may provide you with the inspiration you need to take your dream life further than you ever dreamed possible.

Lucid dream plots are worked out before you go to sleep

The potential for creating a dream scenario is unlimited when you do it advance. Lucid dreamers will use both wake-induced and dream-induced techniques to set up whatever plot they desire for their dreams, no matter how elaborate it may be. And, get this - the more excited you are about that dream, the more likely it will happen. This, alone, is able to yield lucid dreams, by creating scenarios that are ready wired to trigger lucid dreaming. The next time you wonder what it might feel like to go snowboarding down a huge mountain, or sailing round the world in a luxury yacht, even hang gliding over the Grand Canyon, you can do it from the safety of your own bed.

Lucid dreamers can feel themselves flying

If your lucid dream entails you moving, you don't have to walk. You can make yourself glide, or hover, even fly if you want to. When you fly, your whole awareness is pulled into the experience and you will feel as if you are truly flying. Yes, you may worry about falling and then you will fall. That's the way lucid dreaming works – it's up to you, because you're at the controls. But if you maintain the confidence and the expectation that you can fly (try saying out loud, "I'm flying") then you will be successful.

Lucid dreamers get to meet and talk to their heroes

Is there someone in particular who's had a tremendous impact on your life? Maybe that's an author, political figure or historic personality. This person needn't be living; you may have gained a great deal of inspiration and influence from someone who is no longer with us, but that doesn't matter. When you dream lucidly, you can meet and interact with whoever you want and the possibilities are endless. The impact conversations with your heroes can have on your waking life are truly astounding.

Lucid dreamers can summon their dream lovers

Meeting your hero isn't necessarily confined to just talking to them, you know. Lucid dream sex can be extremely satisfying and a fantastic release – you can summon up any lover that you want, be they famous or completely anonymous. For some people, intimacy and sex are great triggers for lucid dreaming because, when they are awake, the only person they expect to be with is their partner. In their dreams, they can be with whoever they want.

Lucid dreamers get to travel through space and time

If you really wanted to clear your mind of all the cobwebs, a trip through space and time is the best thing. Lucid dreamers can travel wherever they wish, in their own private world, visiting new dimensions and go anywhere in time or space they have ever desired to go. You can even hook up with Doctor Who if you want, and become his new assistant for the duration of the dream.

Lucid dreamers can discover new meaning in their lives

Lucid dreams can be used as a way of figuring out what life is all about; a way of putting a personal spin on the meaning of your life. You may discover there is no meaning to it unless you give it one and that's the beauty of lucid dreaming – you can give your life purpose, whether it is for the long term or just a purpose that fascinates you now.

Lucid dreamers can converse with their true inner selves

People who are frequent lucid dreamers have discovered there is something hidden behind their dreams – a new awareness. This awareness is the true inner self of the person dreaming; a wise person who speaks with complete frankness. This is also someone who can reference elements of both the dream and waking life. This is the time to ask yourself all the questions you have ever wanted to, when you were awake, but feared the answers. In your dream space, there's nothing fear. You can freely inquire and explore.

Lucid dreamers can practice their life skills and improve them

While this may sound a little mad, a people attest to the usefulness of this aspect of lucid dream. Stephen LaBerge, in his book *Exploring the World of Lucid Dreaming,* tells the story of a surgeon who has stated that he's rehearsed complex medical procedures scheduled for the next day, in his sleep. He related that it was because of lucid dreaming that he had a reputation for excellence, and could refine his skills and polish his techniques faster than any other surgeon. In a similar way, you can realistically rehearse and practice both emotional and intellectual responses while lucid dreaming, in order to improve your skills in areas you feel need work. These can include public speaking, social skills, skiing, running, or even dancing. Practice really does make perfect and if you can't' do it when you are awake, do it while you sleep.

Lucid dreamers can overcome phobias and fears safely

Let's say that you have a fear of heights. You're not alone. Many people share this fear. When you are lucid dreaming, there is absolutely nothing to stop you from conquering that fear, in total safety. You can climb to the top of the highest mountain, go to the top of the tallest building in the world and peer over the edge, knowing that you're completely safe. If you do fall, you have the ability to slow it all down, transforming your free fall into a gentle float, until you land lightly and safely on the ground. When you have done this a few times in your lucid dreams, you will find that your fears begin to dissipate in real life. You can use this technique to conquer any fear or phobia that have. Dealing with an absolute worst case scenario in your dreams and dealing with it positively, can help create new neural patterns in the unconscious, patterns that can help you to overcome the fear or phobia permanently, in your waking hours.

Lucid dreamers can process grief more easily because they can meet lost loved ones

When we lose someone we love, many of us suffer from a lack of closure. Perhaps you didn't do all the things your wanted to with your loved one, or failed to say everything you wish you had. This is especially true when the loss is sudden or unexpected, but even when we know a loved one's death is imminent, we all wish for another hour or more to sit and talk. In your lucid dreams, you can do just that. Lucid dreams that involve lost loved ones offer a kind of psychological therapy which can amount to closure for those stuck in the grief cycle. Lucid dreaming can make it easier to grieve and to heal and to come to terms with the loss. Lucid dreams can give you the closure that you need to move on with your own life.

Lucid dreamers can explore their creative potential

Lucid dreaming is a fantastic way to improve your creativity. Some people know they have an inner creativity and are too shy to act on it, or struggle to indulge it during waking hours. Lucid dreaming is perfect for nurturing creativity, because your ideas can flow without any hindrance. Creating lucid dreams that inspire your creative spirit can involve asking to see famous works of art, or the beauty of nature. Perhaps you'd like to talk to a famous composer, or experience the wonder of the Sistine Chapel. By consciously calling on your subconscious to help you foster and live out your creativity, you can have access to this neglected inner world.

Lucid dreamers can find worlds that lie beyond the worlds

Lucid dreams consist of a whole range of alternative realities. Whenever you find yourself in a new dream, there will be plenty of odd things going on - lots of new places and landscapes to explore, each one being life like and tangible. Just characters in science fiction films and books do, you can "teleport" yourself from one world to another, visit unknown, alien planets, new dimensions and different historical times. Lucid dreaming allows you to explore the physical universe as your unconscious sees it.

Chapter 6: The Waking Dream

This chapter may be a little more than you bargained for, but since you have come so far already, learning about dreams, nightmares and lucid dreaming, you will also want to know about the biggest one of all – the waking dream. There's a song many of us remember from childhood, that goes, "Row, row, row your boat, gently down the stream. Merrily, merrily, merrily, life is but a dream..." This song is more than just a happy childhood tune. It is a profound lesson in the true nature of our world. It's often said that not resisting the current of life and learning how to go along with the hand that life deals you, or "float downstream", is the true way of happiness and contentment. It's a means of learning certain lessons in life you would otherwise miss out on by always running, headstrong and determined, against life's capricious currents.

Part of what we're going to talk about in this chapter concerns "The Maya", or "The Great Illusion". How often have you had the feeling in your life that you either lived through a situation before, or been someplace you've never been. This sensation is called *déjà vu* (already seen). Many claim to have experienced and while there are varying interpretations of what it means (some of them dismissive scientific theories), it's an oddity that points to a meta-reality of which we're not entirely aware. Most of us know that, as Hamlet says to Horatio in the eponymous Shakespeare play, "There are more things in heaven and earth, Horatio, than are dreamt of in your philosophy". Our dreams are part of this great, subconscious reality, all around us and within us and yet, somehow just beyond our ability to fully grasp its vastness. We know it's there. Some of us call it God, or *logos* (Divine reason at the center of the universe), but no matter what we call it, our awareness of its power is partially linked to the realm of dreams; a place where all is possible.

Jeffery Sumber has said that dreaming is practically irrelevant when it comes to the survival of the human body, but that it's essential in terms of our development and evolution as metaphysical beings. What he means by this is that, in dreams, the laws of physics do not apply. Dreaming is a metaphysical (above the material) reality, not governed by our assumptions about the world, or any existing scientific principle.

Furthermore, Sumber's statement, referring to us as metaphysical beings, takes into account that there is so much more to us than our bodies and brains. The more that we understand ourselves as energetic beings, described in thousand-year-old systems of Traditional Chinese Medicine and Ayurvedic practice in India, the more intimate knowledge we can arrive at concerning our place in the universe. Understanding ourselves as spirit and energy; knowing that our awareness determines our reality, will move us further toward a superior capacity to understand the true nature of our lives and the reality of the world in which we live.

Dreams are a language spoken by our unconscious and through our subconscious. Instead of words or characters, this language works through symbols. While we've discussed how the symbolism in dreams often have universal meanings, dreams provide a very personal experience in which these symbols have highly individualized interpretations and may serve very specialized purposes for the individual dreamer. In other words, these symbols are personal, in addition to the universal significance they bear for dreamers everywhere. Therefore, dreaming as a symbolic language is amorphous, fluid, customized and personalized. This is part of the reason dreams can be so difficult to understand. Coupled with a general inability to adequately apprehend meaning (especially in the West, where introspection and reflection have fallen somewhat out of favor), the individual nature of dream symbolism represents a complex interpretative challenge. This requires an openness on the part of the dreamer, a willingness to explore and reflect on meaning and a focused interest in getting to know what the symbolism in dreams means in terms of the psychological landscape in play.

We use a great deal of symbolic language in the waking world too. For instance, the color red can mean stop. It can also mean passion, fire or anger. It is in our colloquial language, as employed in the phrase, "seeing red" to denote someone who is blind with rage. (The expression refers directly to the use of a red cape in bullfighting to enrage the bull). Think about the hand signals that create a whole other language for the hearing impaired so they can communicate with others. 'Thumbs up' is the universal hand symbol for approval. The cross is widely regarded as a symbol for Jesus and Christianity, while the Star of David is considered to be the symbol for Judaism.

Symbolism gets tricky and becomes confusing for some, because symbols can mean different things to different people. The so-called "rules" for being able to speak this language are, for this reason, difficult to follow as actual rules. The accepted universal definition of certain symbols, however, can serve as guidelines for those hoping to interpret the symbols in dreams can draw on and use as foundations on which to build their personal interpretations. The image of a beer can mean a time for relaxation for some, a time to party for others, something to avoid altogether for recovering alcoholics, and nothing at all to people who have no interest. And so while these symbols become personalized to mean different things to different people, in essence they are still just objects or symbols which carry varying resonances, depending on who's looking at them. They have no meaning until we place significance on them, or cleave to a particular cultural interpretation. This is the basic reason symbols in our dreams are so impervious to global interpretation – they have individual meanings and these meanings are dependent on cultural, social, religious and environmental factors. When we're able to view symbolism from a more neutral and culturally aware perspective, we can begin to see them for what they are –part of a larger, collective dream we're all living out together.

I was talking to my cousin one morning at the breakfast table, eating before going to work. Looking out her kitchen window, she saw two armadillos in the middle of the road in front of her house, having sex. She was quite tickled by scene. Aside from its natural aspects, it's not something one sees every day.

As it was such an unusual event, I felt the impulse, later that day, to look up the meaning of "armadillo" in a dream dictionary. Since it was my cousin who was seeing this event, personally, I emailed her the meaning and asked if it had any significance to her. She responded that evening, saying, "You know, it is funny, but that actually does make a lot of sense!" Apparently, my cousin's marriage was typified, at that time, by some difficulties with her husband. This led to them both being very guarded in their interactions with each other. The "armor" that forms the most distinctive part of the armadillo signifies that guardedness. The fact the armadillos were having sex, symbolized her desire to normalize relations with her husband and return to the marital bliss they had known.

The image of the armadillos triggered a strong reaction that gave way to looking up an interpretation, which actually had significance to my cousin's state of affairs with her husband. Because of the armadillo incident, I began seeking out the interpretations of dream symbolism in connection with other strange occurrences in my life. I rapidly found that many of these provided insight into what was happening in my life at the time. This practice became another piece of the puzzle, revealing the reality of the dream we all live in the midst of. Seeking out meaning in the world that confronts can be a support to understanding why we're here, why things happen and what we should do about them (if anything). I encourage you to try it the next time an odd event or rare occurrence happens. You just might start seeing the world in a new light. Whether that event or occurrence involves armadillos, llamas or platypuses, you never know what the world is trying to tell you. To be quite honest, we're so enmeshed with the world around us, I'd be surprised to hear it wasn't in constant communication with our personal, subconscious world.

With this knowledge, the principles discussed in the chapter on lucid dreaming become even more promising, so start practicing visualization and auto-suggestion techniques to further empower yourself. Make sure you place your focus on something you really want, whether for yourself or others, and put your full intention behind it. Make it something you believe can happen and is beyond any doubt. Start small at first with practical applications. You may be hoping for a successful job interview, picking up a new skill you have been hesitant about learning, or having a stress-free day, if you are used to living with stress. The more you practice and the more results you see, the more you can allow your imagination to expand your horizons and possibilities.

I will leave you with a story universally esteemed throughout generations of philosophers, about an account of a Taoist Zen master whose life was changed forever. This master, Chuang Tzu, had several disciples under his guidance in a temple where he taught his students about living at one with the universe. One night while he was asleep, he had a dream he was a butterfly, flitting from flower to flower, simply enjoying the sensation and experience of being a butterfly. He had no awareness of his individuality as a person. He was a butterfly.

The next day, when Chuang Tzu awoke to find himself a human again, he felt disturbed and had a great look of concern upon his face. He would not eat or drink. His disciples noticed their teacher's sudden change in behavior and asked him, "Master, what is the matter that you choose not to eat or drink? What is this concern of yours that weighs upon you so heavily?" Chuang Tzu told his students about his dream, confessing as to why it concerned him so much. He said, "Now I do not know whether I was then a man dreaming I was a butterfly, or whether I am now a butterfly, dreaming I am a man."

Chapter 7 - Some Amazing Facts About Dreams You Might Not Know

Dreams are mysterious things. They have the power to inform and instruct us, are sometimes bewildering, but always deeply interesting. Through dreams, we can learn about ourselves, the world around us and our places in it.

While we've explored some interesting territory in the land of dreams, here are twenty facts about dreaming you may not have heard before:

You can't tell the time or read while you're dreaming

Some dreams seem so realistic you can't be certain whether you're awake or sleeping. Try, in the midst of a lucid dream, to read text you see as part of the action. Most people can't read anything while in their dream spaces. It's also true that when clocks appear in dreams, they will tell a different time on each occasion you look. Sometimes, the hands won't move at all and the time won't change for the duration of the dream.

Some inventions inspired by dreams

Did you know that dreams are responsible for some of the most important inventions ever known? For example, the following inventions were all developed after the inventor responsible had a dream:

- The idea for the Google search engine came about after Larry Page dreamed about it.
- Tesla invented the alternating current generator following a revelatory dream.
- The double helix spiral form in DNA was identified after James Watson dreamed of it.
- Elias Howe invented a particular sewing machine needle following a nightmare.
- The periodic table was invented by Dimitri Mendeleyev as the result of a dream.

And many more besides.

Some dreams are premonitions

While some scoff at the assertion, many have dreamed of things that actually happened in precisely the way they occurred in a dream. They may have seen only a small glimpse of what was to come, but there is no escaping the fact that premonitions are an interesting (if somewhat controversial) facet of the world of dreams. Some famous premonitions include:

- Abraham Lincoln dreamed of his assassination.
- Many of the 9/11 victims had dreams which warned them about the event.
- Mark Twain dreamed of the death of his brother.
- There are no fewer than nineteen verified

premonition dreams about the sinking of the Titanic.

Dreams which are premonitions of future events can often be so vivid they stay in the dreamer's mind for years afterward. What seems to seal the memory is a combination of familiar, recurring symbols unique to the nature of the promotion, in addition to the playing out of the scenario dreamed in a later event. It's difficult to forget a dream which heralds a waking reality.

Sleepwalking – not as common as you think

Despite the popularity of stories concerning people sleepwalking, it is actually a rare sleep disorder. However, rare it is, it has the potential to be extremely dangerous and is a form of a disorder affecting REM. Sleepwalkers don't stop at acting out what's going on in their dreams though; they head off on real adventures. Take the man who is a nurse by profession; in his dreams he is an artist who can produce fantastic portraits, all drawn while sleeping. The kicker is that he can't remember having created them on awakening. Other strange adventures include:

- A woman who has sex with complete strangers while sleepwalking.
- The man who got in his car, drove for 22 miles and then killed his cousin – all while sleepwalking.

- The sleepwalker who stepped out of a third floor window and barely survived.

Dream catchers are well known symbols

The Dream Catcher is the creation of aboriginal peoples which exists in all individual nations and tribes. These intricate creations serve to symbolically catch dreams and retaining them. They're also said to promote a deep sleep that brings revelatory dreams and prevent nightmares. While there is some controversy about where the dream catcher originates, aboriginal people of the world claim it as their own and not only in Canada and the United States. Examples of it can also be seen in some parts of Latin American, including Mexico.

Dreams increase brain activity

While many people associate sleeping and dreaming with peace, the human brain is at its most active while in a sleep state. This is when the brain does its most intricate and subtle work, sorting out what's happened over the course of the day and filing everything away where it needs to go. Part of this process is dreaming, in which the events of the day and even events from years ago are processed and placed in their proper psychological perspective.

You dream all the time

Some claim they don't dream, but they do. They just don't remember it. Everyone dreams, every night, but around 60% of people will never remember what they dreamed about.

Dreams are negative

On the whole, dreams are negative in orientation. The three most commonly reported emotions experienced during dreaming are anger, fear and sadness. Rarely do you hear of any positive dreams or positive emotions associated with dreams. That it isn't to say that many don't often have positive dreams. The implication is that the negativity experienced in dreams is a subconscious, psychological response to what our brain is telling us about the contents of deepest psychological recesses. It's not always a barrel of laughs in there!

You dream more than once per night

You can actually have up to seven dreams in one night, depending on how many REM cycles your sleep includes. You will only ever dream during the REM sleep stage and, on average, most people have two or three dreams each night. Our dream lives can consume anywhere from 90 minutes to two hours of our sleep, each night.

Chapter 8 - What Your Dreams Can Tell You about Yourself

We all dream. Some more than others. But not many of us actually take advantage of what we learn about ourselves in our dreams. Not everyone can consciously remember the content of the dreams they've had. In many cases, though, the unconscious actually *does* remember. Those of you who remember your dreams should keep a dream journal to write down whatever you can remember of your dreams as soon as you wake up, for later analysis. You may be surprised at how many of those dreams are actually about you. Each separate part of the dream is about a part of you, or your life and relationships. Every dream you have will reveal something about your state of mind in the day or two before you had the dream, generally speaking. Some dreams speak to earlier events, but these are less plentiful than our "sorting" dreams, in which we sift through the detritus of daily life to make of it and decide what our busy minds will retain, for future reference.

What does all this mean? It means that everyone who dreams has an excellent opportunity for self-revelation, to understand their lives and the direction they are moving – all through what you see when you close your eyes at night. Here we look at 10 very useful insights that can help you begin your journey to discovering who you really are and to help you interpret your dreams.

Dreaming about your health

When we dream, the subject matter arises from deep inside us. This is our subconscious mind, reaching out to us. This happens every night, whether you remember it or not. The same thing happens when you meditate, listening to what your intuition is telling you as you concentrate and shut out external distractions. The subconscious mind extracts images from your waking life and transfers them to your dreams, in the form of symbols analogies, or metaphorical actions

While dreams about cars can have many meanings, depending on the variables, these dreams are often about your health. The car is often a symbol of your body. When you're awake, the car is used to transport your body from one place to another becoming, essentially, an extension of your body. The car acts as the vehicle of moving your mind from one place to another. Pay close attention to what state the car in your dream is in. Is it a new car? An old one? Is it damaged or dented in any way? Is it parked, or is it being driven somewhere? When you park your car, you are "resting" it. A parked car in your dream may symbolize that the time has come for some relaxation and rest. If you are the one driving the car, it means you are in full control of your life, but if you're driving and the car is out of control, the symbolism suggests your life may be out of control. When you dream about cars, take a good long look at your health, pay close attention to your body and think about what it could be telling you. As we've stated repeatedly in this book, though, symbolism's significance varies from person to person, so mileage may vary!

Dreaming about your state of mind

Take into account the environmental setting of your dream. That setting reveals the mindset you were in 24 hours before having the dream. If your place of work features, your mind was in working mode, with a focus on accomplishment and activity. If a school appeared in your dreams, you may be focusing on life and the lessons to be learned from it (depending on other factors, in both instances, as always). If you are inside a new house, it may mean you're evolving and perhaps exploring a new way of approaching life. If your dream finds you in the house of your childhood, though, you may be settling into an old and comfortable way of thinking. This may not necessarily be a good thing, as it may signify stubbornness and an unwillingness to change.

Dreaming about how you control your habits

When you dream about animals, you may be dreaming about your personal habits. Animals are habitual, instinctive creatures, and can represent habits and rigid thinking patterns. Some of us have tendencies that cause problems or are addictive, but other habits have a purpose – driving the same way to work every day, brushing your teeth, combing your hair, among the many other daily, repetitive habits we pursue. Look at the animal in your dream and how you are interacting with it. Is the animal a cherished pet or is it an animal you're terrified of? Is the animal on a leash, or is it chasing you across a field or down the street? There are many factors and details that will tell you whether you are controlling your habits, or if they are controlling you. For example, if you dream of an animal chasing you, it can be symbolic of a habit in need of reform. This may point to an addiction, or obsession you need to rid yourself, but avoid addressing in the waking world.

Dreaming about how you connect with your inner self

When you dream about people, are they male, female or a combination of both? When you dream about different sexes, this is a big clue as to how you're connecting with your inner self and the many parts that make up the fullness of you. If you dream about people of the opposite sex, this is a representation of the inner and wise subconscious mind. Dreaming about people of the same sex represents the waking and conscious mind. Think about the people who show up in your dreams. Are you talking to any of them, face to face, or does your interaction take place on the phone? Either way, such interactions are an indication that your conscious and subconscious are communicating in a healthy way. If you're engaged in physical intimacy with the person in your dream, you're connecting very deeply with the part of you (depending on the sex of the person and other elements of the dream) and may be preparing to create something that is completely new, whether an idea or a new aspect of yourself.

What if the people in your dreams are strangers; people you don't know? That means you are not very in touch with that part of yourself. If the dream features a physical struggle, or a chase, you may be fighting with or avoiding a certain part of yourself. Think about what habits you might be trying to avoid working on, or what part of you might be in need of some evolutionary change. The next time you dream someone is chasing you, try to turn around and ask what they want from you – the answer might be illuminating.

Chapter 9 - The Health Benefits of Dreams

Many years of research have now concluded that our dreams are here to help us process strong emotions, consolidate our memories, and tell us things about ourselves. Sometimes, a dream can make a good deal of sense, while other times, a dream may be completely baffling, appearing to make no sense at all. That doesn't mean you should banish the dream from your thoughts entirely. It's still significant to your overall wellbeing and your ability to locate areas that can help you improve that.

One woman, a now retired teacher, can remember very vividly a dream she had almost 40 years earlier. She says she dreamed she was laying on her back, holding on to the rungs of a fireman's ladder, which was fully extended. A boy was right at the top of the ladder, making it sway backwards and forwards as she tried to hold it still. She couldn't manage to achieve this and was terrified the boy would fall. She believes the dream was a symbolic representation of concerns she had in waking reality about trying to teach a boy with severe learning difficulties. She remembers this boy as being one of the most challenging students she had ever taught, and relates that she felt the dream was a nightmare, recalling that it regularly kept her awake most of the night.

This story is an illustration of how our dreams can lead us to understandings about events in our lives that stick with us. They can teach us how to let go of old failures and guilt. In the case of the teacher, who had such difficulty with her challenging, special needs student, years of guilt about her inability to help the boy in the dream have helped her identify something she's been unable to let go of. By looking objectively at the dream and its meaning, she's at least on her way to moving on from the sense of failure and the guilt involved due to her experience of this boy.

Dreams, Memories, and Emotions

The teacher's dream served as a form of auto-therapy. Dreams can have this function in our life, too. That is not to say that some of our dreams may lead us to seek out psychotherapy. This is particularly true of recurring dreams that may be sounding the alarm about repressed memories of child abuse. All the same the self-revelatory function of dreams is an outlet for the things in our lives that stick with us, keeping us awake at night and preventing us from living the fullness of life. Dreams can provide us with a built in coping mechanism and assist us in dealing with unpleasant emotions, memories and psychological burdens.

Dreams occur primarily during REM sleep, during it has been shown that the brain is at its most active. When participants of a sleep study were woken up during their first non-REM stage of the night, those who remembered their dreams reported they had been focusing on an emotional piece of business that was unfinished. During the next REM cycle, the sleepers went on to reshape the problem to restate it in a different way and, as the night wore on, the same thing happened with each cycle. By morning, most reported their problems were now resolved or at least at a manageable state.

Dreaming and Depression

There is no doubt that dreaming has a lot of benefits. According to research done by the National Sleep Foundation, an adult human will spend, on average, two hours per night dreaming. The most vivid and memorable of those dreams will happen during the REM cycle. In a study, rats were deprived of their REM sleep for four days. It was found they produced fewer nerve cells in the hippocampus, which is the memory center of the brain. In humans, dreaming can also help to alleviate the symptoms of depression.

Sleep studies were carried out on women who were recently divorced and who had clinical depression that was not being treated. It was found that the women who remembered their dreams and also incorporated their relationship or their ex-spouse into those dreams, scored much higher on mood tests the following morning. They were also shown to be more likely to recover from their depression than those who did not remember their dreams or who did not include their marriage or ex-spouse in their dreams. What the research also showed was that a lot of work was going on in the brain overnight and that a lot of dream material was working to solve emotional issues.

This activity actively helped lift depression's effects on the study's participants. Going back to the retired schoolteacher - she said that, at the time of the dream, she was in a highly stressed state and the dream made her see how much influence the student had on controlling her life. The problem itself was not solved by the dream, but it was put into a much healthier perspective.

Ways to Derive Health Benefits from Your Dreams

Experts say, following many years of research, that what goes on in our brain overnight can give us insight into how to deal with stress and emotional traumas, as well as improve sleep quality and increase happiness. Dreams can also help solve some of the problems we experience in life. New research suggests that dreams are healthy, and form an important part of the emotional coping process. This is because the thoughts we all encounter which evolve into dreams are a combination of things that have happened recently, of memories that we have buried in our subconscious minds, and of our hopes and fears. Together, they form uniquely dynamic neural connections we would most likely not have access to while awake.

Further research resulted in a report that detailed the results of brain scan studies. These studies showed that the parts of the brain active during the dreaming state share the same qualities as those we use to process emotions and memories while awake. The new thinking on the subject is that dreams help to shape the way you see ourselves, by helping us work through emotions experienced in waking life that remain unresolved. Because of this, even a nightmare can be considered emotionally beneficial. After a significant event in your life, hints of that event will show up in your dreams for up to a week after the event and, because of the recurrence, the presence of these hints can help you to reshape how you understand the event itself.

The health benefits derived from dreaming don't happen all by themselves, though. You need to participate. Following are some tips to help you to fully benefit from the health benefits of dreaming.

Awaken Slowly

The main reason why we forget our dreams is because your superego works hard to protect your conscious mind from any disturbing and upsetting images that may have been brought up by the unconscious, as you slept. While that may sound great in theory, especially if you are plagued by nightmares, in reality you need to remember your dreams if you want to use them to help yourself.

When you wake in the morning, stay in the exact position you found yourself when you woke up and keep your eyes shut. Do not let your mind wander to what is ahead of you for the day. It takes only 90 seconds for your brain to wipe out all memories of your dream and, when that is gone from your mind, so are the potential benefits. When you have remembered everything you can about your dream, write it down in your dream journal. Keep this with a pen, on the nightstand next to your bed. A dedicated dream journal is preferable to a pad of paper or stack of post-its. It's permanent and it honors its purpose by being specifically for recording your dreams and no other purpose. Later on, go back to what you wrote and read it, reflecting on what the dream might have meant. Pay attention to any recurring patterns and look for symbolic references rather than literal ones.

Don't Read Your Dreams Literally

It really doesn't help you arrive at an insight if you read your dreams literally. Just because you dream that you partner has cheated on you, it doesn't mean they have and it doesn't even mean you're concerned they might. What it may indicate is that you're concerned about the amount of time your partner spends away from you, at work. It can also mean your partner is always distracted, or that your relationship needs some work. Be a little loose when it comes to interpreting your dreams and again, look for that symbolic reference, not the literal.

Practice Dream Intervention

For some who have the same nightmare night after night, this could be the solution. Instead of letting whatever it is that bothering you (as indicated by a recurring nightmare) win, learn how to intervene in the dream. One man who dreamed a toy car was chasing him finally learned how to do this. In the dream, he intervened - he stopped, turned around and told the car to go away. The car slowed down, became something that was no longer a menace and eventually turned into exactly what it was – an inanimate toy car. Since then, this man has been able to intervene in a number of nightmares and stop them. He's also been able to stop himself from falling in dreams, transforming falling into flying. It is important that when you intervene in your dreams, you do so only when things become too much because otherwise, you could be missing out on some important messages.

People who endure traumatic or stressful experiences in their lives tend to relive them in dreams or nightmares. Many of these people go on to successfully learn how to intervene in their dreams and can take control of subconscious messages and images. You can learn how to change the direction your dream is going in and you can also get to the stage at which you can ask the dream itself what message it is trying to give you. When you are going to bed, before you go to sleep, remember the dream or the theme that continues to show up when you sleep, and think of ways to change the course of it. Think of things you can do in your waking life to combat whatever is showing up in your sleep as a nightmare. One of those ways is to seek the assistance of a clinical professional, particularly if the recurring dream or nightmare is keeping you awake, interfering with your work or relationships, or otherwise damaging your ability to function. There are times when these dreams are telling you something you need the help of a professional to explore further.

Play All the Characters in Your Dream

According to Freud, every character is in our dreams is a representation of ourselves. This can be quite useful, as it's possible to imagine yourself as each individual character.

Let's say a recurring theme in your dream is a massive tree is blowing in the wind. Imagine you are the tree and ask yourself what your role is as that tree. Do you have a purpose? How does it feel to be the tree? Are there any limitations or joys connected to being a tree? Think about the fixed nature of a tree, rooted to the earth. Do you feel stuck? Are you sensing that you're not where you want to be and feel powerless to change that? You may find that your feelings are related to those of being rooted and strong, but you might also find that you are very limited. Think about that in direct relation to something that may be going on in your life right now.

Summarize the Dream

When you do this, give the dream a title, as if it were a novel or movie. Focus on what that title tells you, as it points to which aspects of the dream were important enough to define its character and lead you to choose the title. Another exercise, according to Reneau Peurifoy, MORE ON THIS GUY a dream interpretation expert, is to imagine you are having a conversation with someone new to the planet earth (an alien). How would you describe your dream to that alien so it made sense? Which parts of it would you emphasize and why? Write all these observations down, because this is a good way of recalling the details and of focusing on aspects you may have overlooked, but which may be important. This will also help you interpret dream symbols more properly to arrive at better insights.

Let Your Dreams Guide You

Once you begin to remember more of your dreams and understand them more fully, you can work on identifying the emotions or events in your life which are influencing or inspiring your dreams. That way, you can sort out how to intellectually process those parts of your life causing you emotional upheaval. If your dreams don't really have endings, or you weren't happy with the ending you got, think about how you would like it to have ended. Think about how you can manipulate the outcome of your dreams by making the appropriate changes in your life. Think about how some of your dreams are resolved and ask yourself if these were practical. Were they healthy resolutions? Listen to what your dreams are telling you. Use your dreams to identify connections you wouldn't normally have thought of, then let your dreams guide you toward making the appropriate changes in your waking life.

Chapter 10 – Frequently Asked Questions About Dreams

To finish off and recap what I have already gone over, following are some of the more commonly asked questions about dreams.

How many dreams do we have in one night?

On average, a person will have between three and five dreams every night, although some people will dream up to seven times a night. Dreams tend to start short and grow longer as the night progresses. If you sleep a full 8 hours, you'll dream for approximately two of those hours. When you go to sleep, you move through four different stages of sleep throughout the course of the night. It is in the last of those four stages, the REM cycle, that you'll dream. Each of the sleep cycles lasts between 60 and 90 minutes and then, when the fourth cycle is complete, the cycle returns to the beginning, on a continuous loop until you wake up. The longer you sleep, the more dreams you will have.

Why don't some people dream?

Everyone dreams and this has been proven scientifically. In a large study carried out WHERE, all the people enrolled showed brain activity while sleeping and that equates to dreaming. The reason some people say they don't dream is they can't remember their dreams. The reasons for this are various – the level of alcohol consumed before sleep, antibiotics you may be taking, a fever, not enough sleep or, quite simply, too much sleep. Even high stress levels or a fear, conscious or subconscious, about your dreams, may block you from remembering them. Some researchers say there are people who are genetically disposed to forget their dreams as soon as they wake up.

What is the difference between adult and child dreams?

Do they have the same significance? No, because our dreams reflect the experiences we have had and any life concerns we're currently undergoing. Children up to the age of about five don't really have a storyline to their dreams, nor is there any strong emotional content. However, children of this age are more likely to have a nightmare related to childhood fears – monsters under the bed, school, strangers, loud noises and other disturbing phenomenon. By the time a child becomes a teenager, their dreams will more closely match those of adults, simply because their concerns, fears and emotions have evolved.

Can dreams predict the future?

While there isn't any scientific proof that dreams can foretell what is going to happen, some people do have precognitive dreams. They will dream something in vivid detail that may come true later on. The only way to explain this is to say that these dreams are a result of information gathering. Our subconscious and conscious minds work together, picking up information and consolidating into a dream. This is done subconsciously and it means that, deep down, you already knew it was going to happen and it just looks as though your dream predicted it. Another explanation is that some of these dreams are coincidence. Finally, the possibility of premonitions being part of our dreamscapes is not out of the question. As Shakespeare wrote, there is more in heaven and earth (than we can possibly know about).

Why do we dream?

There is a great deal of research into this, but it's most commonly believed that dreams are a way for our minds to cleanse us and release emotions. Throughout your normal day, you probably hold back a certain amount of emotion, perhaps anger or sadness at something that has happened. That emotion builds up inside you and, when you sleep, your body relaxes and your brain gets to work. Dreams are one of the safest ways to release all that pent up emotion safely. There is another theory that says dreams are a necessary part of sleep in a biological sense. Research shows that people who are stopped from entering into the REM stage of sleep, thus not being able to dream, are irritated more easily, more jittery and exhibit a lower than average performance in their daily lives.

Are our dreams significant in any way?

Yes, all dreams have significance (although not all researchers and scientists agree on this point). Every dream contains images that are symbols and have hidden meanings which go way beyond what you actually see in your dreams. You must remember not to take what you see in your dreams literally. Rather, you should look for the symbols and work out the meaning of your dream, using universal interpretations of these symbols as a guide. The significance of your dreams is personal to you and your life experiences, referring to what you may be enduring in life at the time and your emotional state. However, that said, there are a lot of universal symbols so note your dreams every time you remember them and look for the symbols and patterns using the universal interpretation as a guide, but not as a hard and fast rule.

Is it significant if I dream of the same person over and over again?

It could be that the person you continually dream of is on your mind a lot in your waking life. Your dream may be telling you that you have to let this person know your feelings, especially if the dream is a good one. It may be telling you that, by letting that person know your feelings, only good things can come from it. If the person is not interested, at least you will know that you can move on with your life. The person you're dreaming of may also represent another type of wish or goal. As stated above, it's important to analyze all aspects of your dreams, particularly if they recur. The recurrence of a person in your dreams may have multiple meanings which may be interpreted by examining an overview of all factors and symbols implicated.

Why do some particular dreams repeat themselves?

Recurring dreams are an indication there's an issue in your life you are not dealing with; an issue that needs to be resolved. You may have anxieties and high stress levels about particular issues and these can also cause dreams to repeat themselves. When this happens, it is time to take a long hard look at your life and work out what needs to be resolved before you can move on. If the nature of the recurring dream frightens or disturbs you to the point of dysfunction or anxiety, it's probably advisable to seek the support of a clinical professional. Recurring dreams can point to repressed memories you should explore. Another possibility is PTSD, in which case clinical consultation is strongly advised.

Do we dream in color or in black and white?

Most people dream in color, but a certain percentage of the population will dream only in black and white. Color is a natural part of our lives, something we see every day but because we take it for granted, we don't always notice color in our dreams. Another reason people don't remember dreaming in color is that their memory recall skills are poor and dreams fade very quickly. This effect occurs within 90 seconds of waking and we may only be able to recall the dream in gray shades. Some dreams which are only in black and white could be an indication of depression or sadness in your life.

Do dreams reflect our intelligence levels?

Some people say that if your dreams allow you to experience vibrant sensory phenomenon, such as color and detail, touch, smell and taste, it indicates that you enjoy higher intelligence. This has not been proven scientifically. Dreams come from deep within your subconscious and what we see is an expression of our emotions and inner selves. Dreaming is highly personal, varies from person to person, but may, indeed, correlate to intelligence. In fact, researchers have found that the frequency with which we dream is a stronger indicator of IQ, with people of high IQ dreaming more frequently with those of lower intelligence quotient. As stated above, though, science has still not arrived at a satisfactory answer in this regard.

Does my dog dream?

Yes. All animals dream because, in the same way as human beings, their brain activity increases overnight. You've probably noticed your pet moving its legs in its sleep or making noises. This indicates that your pet is dreaming. However, the nature of their dreams is unknown because we can't actually ask them!

What is REM sleep?

REM, or rapid eye movement sleep is the fourth stage of the sleep cycle and is the part of that cycle in which you achieve the deepest sleep. The reason this is called rapid eye movement is that, during this stage of sleep, your eyes move backwards and forwards beneath your eyelids in rapid movements. It is also in the REM stage that you most commonly dream and which you may experience the most vivid dreams and, on occasion, the most bizarre dreams.

How do our daily lives affect our dreams?

Throughout the day, we suppress certain emotions, whether we realize we're doing it or not. Those feelings stand a good chance of being released through your dreams although, typically, some of them can take a couple of days to come out. Sometimes, we continue to dream about events and people in our lives for months or years. If, for example, you have feelings of anger toward someone but have held them in check, not revealing or acknowledging within 24 to 48 hours, that anger could manifest itself in your dreams, usually in a symbolic way. Trauma or stress can also affect your dreams.

Do men and women dream differently?

Yes and no. In terms of dream patterns, they don't. Brain activity is the same in both men and women but the content of the dreams can be different. As stated repeatedly in this book, dreams are highly personal and individualized and that applies to both sexes equally. But research has determined that men tend to feature more men in their dreams, while women dream about both men and women, equally. This makes sense when you consider that dreams are reflections of our deepest self-identities. If a man dreams about a woman, it is an indication that he is expressing the feminine side of his nature. Let's face it. Not many men want to admit to themselves that they have a softer, more feminine side, which is an unfortunate reality of the male psyche, rooted in insecurity concerning their masculinity. Women don't tend to labor under the same type of self-regulation concerning gender and its meaning.

I only remember nightmares, not dreams. Is this normal?

It really isn't a question of what is normal. It's more a question of why you only remember the nightmares and not the dreams. Nightmares tend to be easier to remember, for a number of reasons. First of all, they are much more vivid and frightening. A nightmare is more likely to jolt you from sleep. If you wake up during the REM stage of sleep, you are more likely to remember what you dreamed. Secondly, nightmares usually happen in the early morning hours, just as you are about to awaken. Remembering dreams is not about normality. In the world of dreams, everything and nothing is normal, but remember them is entirely about the effort you put into retaining the information they provide.

I dreamed in my dream. What does this mean?

When you dream within your dream, it's considered a safer way to express the stuff of your unconscious. A dream that happens in a dream is protecting you from waking up, in essence. Dreams within dreams very often hold a deep, hidden meaning which reflects a crucial issue you need to confront and resolve.

Can you "die" in your dreams?

It is perfectly possible to experience death when you dream. Dreams of your own death are normally the result of a high level of stress, caused by a number of factors, including: sweeping life changes, relationships which have ended, school, your children growing up, the loss of a job, a failure or generalized anxiety about death. Death in dreams is normally seen as a symbol that something is happening; something is changing, and it isn't necessarily a bad thing. Some people say that if you die in your dreams you never wake up. This is a folkloric claim which is not based in fact.

Can we talk to people in our dreams?

It is perfectly possible to connect with other people in our dreams, but only on a symbolic level. When you dream about talking to other people, it's more of a rehearsal for what you want to say to the person in your waking life. If that person has already passed from this life, this type of dream is generally a reflection of the things you wanted to say to them, but didn't have the opportunity to. Dreams can help you connect with people and can often show you the way to approach them. As to whether it's possible for two people to hold an actual conversation in a dream, that's still the subject of much research. This is known as dream telepathy and is a form of a paranormal or psychic dream. There are the stories of those who are close, such as mothers and their children, or twins, being able to communicate via their dreams. To date there is no scientific data to support this possibility.

Sometimes do we sometimes awaken with a start from a dream?

There is a scientific term for this - myoclonic jerks. Sometimes people dream they are falling and they twitch or jerk their arms or legs as a physiological response, waking themselves up in the process. There is no real reason for this, but one theory is that it's an instinctive response to a situation the brain sees as potentially dangerous. On occasion, dreams seem so real that the brain genuinely believes you're in danger; that you are falling. This provokes a fight or flight response, which prompts the jerkiness and twitching of your body, or a hypnic jerk.

Why can't we all remember our dreams?

Some people remember every dream they have ever had, while others can't remember a single one, or will only remember the occasional dream. Virtually everything you see in your sleep; everything that happens while you are asleep, is forgotten by the time morning arrives. The phenomenon of sleep makes it difficult to remember what you dreamed about unless you write it down as soon as you wake up. Don't forget, most dreams are gone from the mind within 90 seconds of waking, although dream fragments may come back to you over the course of the day. This suggests that the memory has not been wiped out, only filed away in a place in which it can't be retrieved very easily. Some people may not remember a dream when they wake up, but something will happen later on, or the next day that can trigger the memory of the dream.

Other things that can affect your ability to remember your dreams are drugs and alcohol. Ceasing to take certain medications can actually induce nightmares, so you should discuss medication concerns with your doctor.

Can I improve my dream memory?

Yes. Before you fall asleep, tell yourself that you want to remember what you dream about. Have a dream diary, a pen and paper or a tape recorder beside your bed. When you wake up, don't move from the position you are in. Lay there with your eyes closed and try not to think about anything. Write down or record everything you remember of your dream. If you don't do this quickly, the memory will fade. If anything distracts you, the memories will disappear. If you can't remember the whole dream, just write down everything that you can, even if it is only a vague memory.

Can I learn how to interpret my dreams?

Yes, you can, but you must bear in mind that what you dream about is usually a reflection of your own state of mind, your feelings and emotions. The people in your dreams, the actions and the settings, even the emotions, are all personal to you. There are universal dream themes, symbols, or elements of dreams experienced by many different people, no matter where they are in the world, or what their culture is. However, each time a symbol is seen in a dream, it will have a different meaning for the person who is dreaming about it. For example, the symbol of a cross, dreamed by ten people will have ten different meanings. While the symbol may be universal, its interpretation can vary wildly. That means taking into account all elements about the dream you can remember, as well as situations they may refer to, in order to attempt an interpretation relevant to you.

Are nightmares normal?

Among younger children, nightmares are very common and they are also fairly common in adults too. Nightmares tend to be caused by stress, emotional problems, traumatic experiences, medications, drugs or an illness. Some people tend to have nightmares on a regular basis. Studies have suggested that some people who have nightmares are more sensitive, open, trusting and emotional than the average person.

Can I control my dreams?

You can give yourself what are known as pre-sleep suggestions as a way of influencing what you dream about. Another popular method of controlling your dreams is lucid dreaming. In lucid dreaming, you are fully aware you are dreaming, as you sleep and can experience some pretty amazing things. You can also create a dream sequence before you go to sleep and then experience it. For some people, lucid dreaming is spontaneous. You can learn how to increase the likelihood of lucid dreaming, and you can also learn how to affect the course your dream takes. However, not everything is easy to control and some aspects of your dreams will be completely beyond yours. It is important to remember that, even if you are dreaming lucidly, there will still be certain symbols and meanings related to your waking life. Some researchers suggest it isn't advisable to attempt to control your dreams, and that you should relax and learn how to enjoy your ludic dreams, as well as using them to make changes for the better in your waking life.

Dreams can be used to help you to improve your life, health and relationships, or to make you see there are certain realities in your life and personality which require reform. While it isn't always possible to, you should try to relax as much as you can before retiring. This will put you in the best possible place to enjoy your dreams and give the best chance of remembering them when you awaken.

Remember not to take the content of your dreams too literally. Dreams are rarely literal. They are generally very symbolic, so learn what those symbols mean, in universal terms, and relate them to what's happening in your life, stresses you're challenged by and situations you're struggling with that need resolution. That's the only way to truly understand your dreams and what they mean.

Conclusion

Thank you for purchasing this book.

There are many theories concerning dreams and what they mean. But the universal nature of dreams means that they're of interest to all of us. We all dream! While the study of what goes on inside our heads in our sleep has evolved through time and continues to evolve, even today, the subject has always been a point of keen interest for those of us who are fascinated by the workings of the mind, particularly those of the subconscious. As we learn more than Freud or Jung could have ever hoped to know (regardless of their enormous contributions to the subject), we're becoming increasingly able to interpret the role of dreams in our waking lives, and how they support our overall mental and physical wellbeing. We're discovering that they can take us to worlds our open eyes will never see. We're also discovering how they can provide a window on our subconscious, secret lives and what that means to our personal evolution, as individuals.

In learning more about interpreting our dreams and lucid dreaming, we're giving ourselves the gift of insight into our innermost beings. Despite Jung's assertion that the subconscious and conscious minds are bridged, in dreams, of their own accord and without an interpretative support, putting some energy into interpretation is a journey of self-exploration. By actively investigating the content of our dreams and seeking to remember and analyze it, we crossing Jung's bridge with conscious steps, toward obtaining a better grasp of what's on the other side of it. It's there, so why not cross it? Why not reach out for the self-knowledge and personal enlightenment that lies across the turbulent waters of our sleeping minds?

Because it's across that bridge that our most poignant and deeply felt stories are to be experienced. Healing from past trauma and hurts is on that side of the bridge. Knowledge about our more inexplicable triggers, too. Repressed memories, forgotten events (including the ghost of Christmases past, no doubt) can be found crouching there, in the reeds of the subconscious.

By fostering an awareness of what goes on in your head in sleep, you will be more readily able to recognize the significance of your actions and their triggers in waking life. Establishing a dream journal to record whatever you can remember about your dreams is the first step in making your dreams work for you. By recording and analyzing them and periodically examining the contents of your journal, you can begin to understand what universal dream symbols mean to you, personally.

Particularly for those who are suffering from anxiety and trauma, dream interpretation and analysis can be valuable tools toward arriving at a place of healing. Those who suffer from depression or who are recovering from Post-Traumatic Stress Disorder with the help of a therapist, can find abundant benefit in this discipline. The study of dream interpretation's history and place in world cultures is a fine and worthy support for this type of personal development work. This is a human activity which is not "oddball" or a pseudo-science. Dream interpretation and analysis have a history stretching thousands of years into the past. Humanity's interest has always been keen and while it may have fallen out of fashion in these technocratic times, clearly, there's still a need for it and interest in it.

While some readers may find the proposition fantastical or even laughable, the truth is that lucid dreaming has been recognized as a reality by primitive cultures around the world for eons. The West's skepticism in its confrontation may well stem from the influence of European religion and its more controlling aspects. I don't expect the local priest or pastor thinks much of the idea of people being able to control their dreams, without a priestly mediator. Nor do I expect the clergy is particularly fond of the idea that our dreams aren't always messages from the Almighty. But as I've tried to demonstrate here, lucid dreaming is a very real thing, accessible to anyone interesting in conscientiously and consistently pursuing it. Dreaming lucidly can be the gateway to a richer life, with a greater understanding of who we are and, as a result, a greater understanding of our role and purpose in the universe. Joseph Campbell admonished us to "follow (our) bliss". How much more profoundly and thoroughly might we heed that admonition with the ability to dream the dreams we most wish to. Could that ability not inform many of us about the bliss we're missing out on?

Whatever your disposition is toward dream interpretation, or lucid dreaming, I hope I've been able to make it all seem a little less "new age" to you. As you have read, there's nothing "new" about the world of dreams. Dreaming is a human reality common to us where ever we are and whoever we are. It's a binding thread in the human experience which can be made richer and a more active part of our lives, if we'll only take the time to explore the possibilities it presents.

Thank you again for buying this book, I hope that you have enjoyed reading it.

Bonus

Who can dream without a good night's sleep? Learn ways to sleep better, quickly! As my passion is sharing valuable information that tangibly impacts your life (be it learning how to dream properly or otherwise), I'd like to invite you to the free bonus below to positively affect your life in other dimensions, and join my mailing list where I drip-feed free information that I think may be of benefit to you (zero spam ever).

If you want to take your health to the next level, I recommend the free resource below for some easy-to-follow quick tips that make a huge impact.

23 Health Tips & Hacks You Probably Aren't Doing But Should Be to Reduce Fatigue, Improve Sleep and Recovery, Boost Sex Drive, and Heal Your Gut

Visit https://publishfs.leadpages.co/getultrahealth/

Made in the USA
Columbia, SC
02 August 2018